Without Touch of Dishonour

Sir Henry Slingsby, aet. 53, from the portrait in Lacock Abbey where it hangs with the portraits of his daughter, Barbara, and her husband, Sir John Talbot. The inscription below the window is described in Appendix II (page 182).

(By permission of Mrs Burnett Brown of Lacock Abbey.)

Without Touch of Dishonour

The Life and Death of Sir Henry Slingsby

1602 — 1658

Geoffrey Ridsdill Smith

with an Introduction by
Brigadier Peter Young, DSO, MC, MA, FRSA, FR Hist S

Kineton : The Roundwood Press
1968

First published on 8th June, 1968

SBN 900093 01 3

Set in 'Monotype' Caslon, series 128 and printed by
Gordon Norwood at The Roundwood Press, Kineton, in the County of Warwick.
Bound by Henry Brooks at Oxford.
Plates made by The Process Engraving Company of Coventry.

Made and printed in England

Genio Loci

Contents

Illustrations

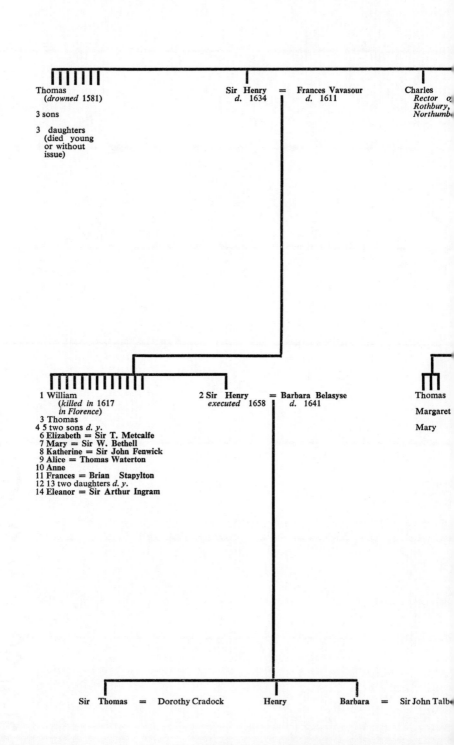

Thomas
(*drowned* 1581)

3 sons

3 daughters
(died young
or without
issue)

Sir Henry = Frances Vavasour
d. 1634   d. 1611

Charles
*Rector of
Rothbury,
Northumb*

1 William
(*killed in* 1617
in Florence)
3 Thomas
4 5 two sons *d. y.*
6 Elizabeth = Sir T. Metcalfe
7 Mary = Sir W. Bethell
8 Katherine = Sir John Fenwick
9 Alice = Thomas Waterton
10 Anne
11 Frances = Brian Stapylton
12 13 two daughters *d. y.*
14 Eleanor = Sir Arthur Ingram

2 Sir Henry = Barbara Belasyse
executed 1658   d. 1641

Thomas

Margaret

Mary

Sir Thomas = Dorothy Cradock   Henry   Barbara = Sir John Talbot

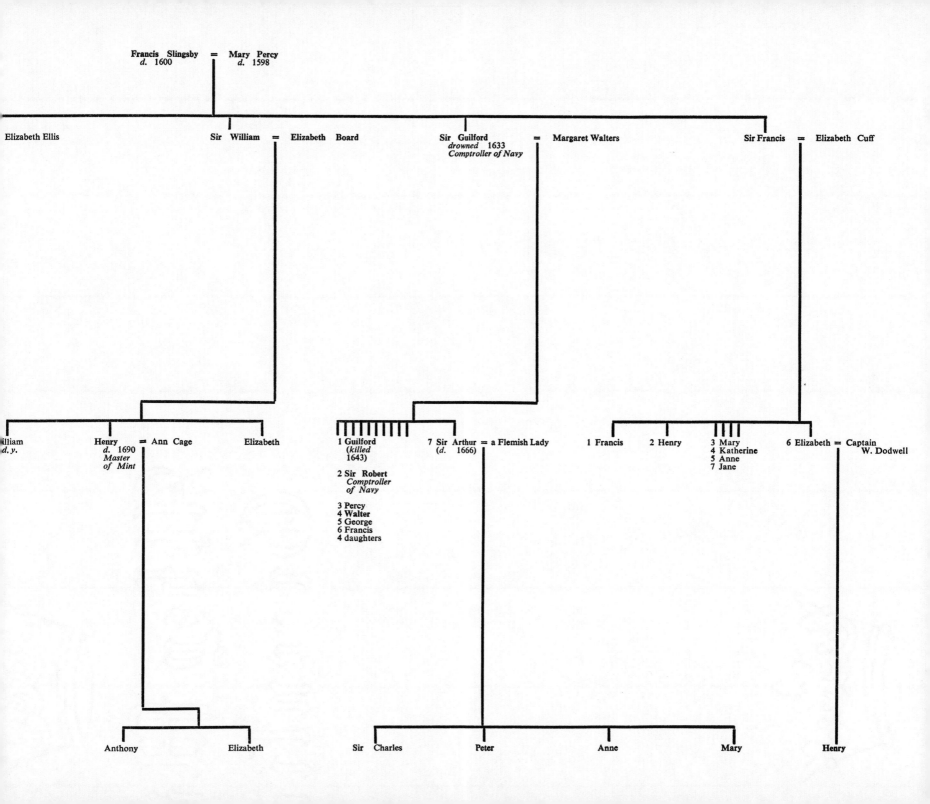

Francis Slingsby = Mary Percy
d. 1600   *d.* 1598

Elizabeth Ellis

Sir William = Elizabeth Board

Sir Guilford = Margaret Walters
drowned 1633
Comptroller of Navy

Sir Francis = Elizabeth Cuff

William
d. y.

Henry = Ann Cage
d. 1690
*Master
of Mint*

Elizabeth

1 Guilford
(*killed*
1643)

2 Sir Robert
*Comptroller
of Navy*

3 Percy
4 **Walter**
5 George
6 Francis
4 daughters

7 Sir Arthur = a Flemish Lady
(*d.* 1666)

1 Francis

2 Henry

3 Mary
4 Katherine
5 Anne
7 Jane

6 Elizabeth = Captain
W. Dodwell

Anthony

Elizabeth

Sir Charles

Peter

Anne

Mary

Henry

Acknowledgements

Without Brigadier Peter Young's ready help and encouragement this book, which he has befriended with an Introduction, might never have been written, and I am deeply indebted to him. Also to Mr C. W. Crawley of Trinity Hall, for reading the typescript, and to Mr Martin Hooton for reading the proofs, and for their kindly and constructive criticism. Mrs G. S. Brunskill, who worked on the Slingsby papers for a number of years and saved some that might otherwise have been lost, has generously put at my disposal the results of her work. Professor David Underdown, writing from the University of Virginia, suggested fresh lines of research and his 'Royalist Conspiracy in England' proved a racy and indispensable guide to this hitherto neglected decade. Mr B. N. Reckitt, with his intimate knowledge of 17th century Hull, solved several of my problems, as did Colonel Henry Slingsby on points of family history. Professor A. H. Woolrych introduced me to fruitful sources of information, and his study of Yorkshire's part in the Restoration helped me to round off my story. With Mr F. J. Routledge I have enjoyed a lengthy correspondence sorting out the various Slingsbys who crop up in the Calendar of the Clarendon State Papers which he has edited. To Mr A. E. B. Owen of the University Library, Cambridge, I owe the deciphering of the all but indecipherable handwriting of Slingsby's tutor, the Rev. Phatuel Otby, as well as the transcription of the much damaged Marston Moor letter. My one-time colleague at Redhouse, Mr T. E. Hardwick who, as its headmaster, experienced many of Slingsby's own problems in running the house and estate, has frequently come to my aid. Likewise his successor, Mr P. G. Spencer, one of whose aims is to restore Redhouse to its rightful place in history.

ABBREVIATIONS

ADD. MS.   Additional Manuscripts, British Museum.

BM.   British Museum

CARTE.   A Collection of Original Letters and Papers concerning the Affairs of England ... 1641 to 1660, found among the Duke of Ormond's Papers.

CCC.   Calendar of the Proceedings of the Committee for Compounding, ed. M. A. E. Green.

C CL S P   Calendar of the Clarendon State Papers, ed. O. Ogle, W. H Bliss, W. D. Macray and F. J. Routledge.

CLARENDON CON   The Life of Edward Clarendon ... in which is included Continuation of his History of the Grand Rebellion.

CLARENDON HISTORY   Edware Hyde: The History of the Rebellion and Civil Wars in England, ed. W. D. Macray.

CL S P   State Papers Collected by Edward, Earl of Clarendon, ed. R. Scrope and T. Monkhouse.

CSPD   Calendar of State Papers, Domestic Series, ed. M. A. E. Green.

DNB   Dictionary of National Biography.

EHR   English Historical Review.

HMC   Historical Manuscripts Commission Report.

RAWL MSS.   Rawlinson MSS. (Bodleian)

SPDI   State Papers Domestic, Interregnum (Public Record Office).

TSP   A Collection of State Papers of John Thurloe, Esq.

Dramatis Personae

FRANCIS SLINGSBY *and his wife* MARY PERCY

SIR HENRY the Elder ⎫
SIR WILLIAM ⎪
SIR GUILFORD ⎬ *their sons*
SIR FRANCIS ⎭

SIR HARRY, *son to* SIR HENRY the Elder
BARBARA BELASYSE, *his wife*

THOMAS ⎫
HENRY ⎬ *their children*
BARBARA ⎭

HENRY SLINGSBY, *alias* 'Samborne', *son to* SIR WILLIAM

COLONEL GUILFORD ⎫
SIR ROBERT ⎪
COLONEL WALTER ⎬ *sons to* SIR GUILFORD
SIR ARTHUR ⎭

1st VISCOUNT FAUCONBERG, SIR HARRY's *father-in-law*
HENRY BELASYSE, *his eldest son*
JOHN BELASYSE, *his second son*
2nd VISCOUNT FAUCONBERG, *his grandson*
MARY CROMWELL, *the 2nd Viscount's wife*

JOHN PRESTON, *Tutor of Queens' College*

SIR THOMAS FAIRFAX, *friend and neighbour, C-in-C Parliamentary forces*
SIR MARMADUKE LANGDALE ⎫
SIR JOHN MAYNEY ⎬ *comrades in arms, royalist army*

MAJOR ROBERT WALTERS ⎫
CAPTAIN JOHN WALTERS ⎬ *royalist agents*
MAJOR NICHOLAS ARMORER ⎭

COLONEL HENRY SMITH, *Governor of Hull Castle*
MAJOR RALPH WATERHOUSE ⎫
CAPTAIN JOHN OVERTON ⎬ *officers of the garrison*
LIEUT. GEORGE THOMPSON ⎭

xi

NATIONAL EVENTS	YEAR	FAMILY EVENTS
Domesday Survey	1086	Manor of Scarchetorp (Scagglethorpe) held by Osbern de Arcis who, with his wife Ivetta, founded Nun Monkton Priory in Stephen's reign
	1300	Sir Robert Ughtred, probable builder of the first Redhouse, granted free warren in Moor Monkton and Scagglethorpe
Edward I's Scottish Wars	1301	Sir Robert commissioned to select 1100 foot for Scottish War
Edward I dies	1307	Sir Robert dies
Edward II's Scottish War, Bannockburn	1314	Sir Thomas Ughtred at Bannockburn
	1319	Sir Thomas, Commissioner of Array for Yorkshire – served at siege of Berwick
	1320	Knight of the Shire for Yorkshire
Edward III supports Balliol	1332	Sir Thomas at Balliol's coronation – sits in Scottish parliament as Lord Ughtred
Rising against Balliol, who flees	1334	Lord Ughtred holds Roxburgh Bridge and so secures Balliol's withdrawal. He is licensed to impark his woods
100 Years War	1339	Ughtred, at siege of St. Omer, with his archers defeats the French
	1342	He is licensed to crenellate Redhouse
Crecy	1346	He fights at Crecy
Treaty of Bretigny	1360	He is made a Knight of the Garter
	1365	He dies and Thomas succeeds to Le Rede Howse and six other manors
Black Prince's expedition to Spain	1366	Thomas Ughtred fights in French and Scottish Wars
	1487	Thomas's great-grandson, Henry, lends Redhouse to Joseph Ughtred
Henry VIII succeeds	1509	Henry Ughtred knighted by Henry VIII
Field of the Cloth of Gold	1520	Robert, Sir Henry's son, sells Redhouse to Sir Anthony Ughtred, his uncle, who had been made Marshal of Tournai after the Battle of the Spurs. He married Elizabeth Seymour, Jane Seymour's sister
War with France	1523	Robert Ughtred knighted on the banks of the Somme

NATIONAL EVENTS	YEAR	FAMILY EVENTS
	1531	Sir Anthony sells Redhouse to his brother-in-law, Sir Edward Seymour, retaining the right to live there till his death
Henry VIII marries Jane Seymour. Pilgrimage of Grace	1536	Sir Thomas Percy, Francis Slingsby's father-in-law, executed for taking part in the Pilgrimage of Grace
Treaty of Edinburgh between England and Scotland	1560	Sir Edward Seymour sells the reversion of Redhouse to Francis Slingsby
	1572	7th Earl of Northumberland, Francis Slingsby's brother-in-law, executed for plotting in favour of Mary Queen of Scots
	1581	Thomas, Francis's eldest son, drowned in the Nidd
Throgmorton's Plot	1584	
	1585	8th Earl of Northumberland, Francis's brother-in-law implicated in Throgmorton's Plot, shot himself in the Tower
	1595	Henry Slingsby, now the eldest son, buys Redhouse
Expedition to Cadiz	1596	William and Guilford, Henry's brothers, on the Cadiz expedition
	1600	Francis Slingsby dies
	1601	Henry and William M.P.'s for Knaresborough
	1602	Henry knighted by Mountjoy in Dublin Castle
Gunpowder Plot	1605	Sir Henry investigates suspects in Yorkshire. 9th Earl of Northumberland, his cousin, imprisoned in the Tower
	1606	Sir Henry signs a contract for burning of bricks to build a new Redhouse
	1607	Building begun. Harry, his second son, goes to school at Foston, aged 6
	1610	William, his eldest son, goes to complete his education in France
	1611	Sir Henry's wife, Frances, dies
	1613	William goes to Italy
	1617	William is killed in Florence
Thirty Years War	1618	Harry goes up to Cambridge
	1621	Harry goes abroad with his Tutor, John Preston

NATIONAL EVENTS	YEAR	FAMILY EVENTS
	1629	Sir Henry appointed Vice President of the Council of the North by Wentworth
	1631	Harry marries Barbara Belasyse
Charles I visits Scotland	1633	Charles I stays at Redhouse. Barbara, Harry's first child, born
	1634	Sir Henry dies
Ship Money writs	1636	Thomas, the second child, born at Redhouse
Signing of the Covenant	1638	Harry starts his Diary, and is made a Baronet of Novia Scotia. Birth of third child, Henry
First Scots War	1639	Sir Harry takes View of Arms: joins Lord Holland on the Border
The Long Parliament. Second Scots War, Newcastle captured	1640	Sir Harry (henceforth to be called Slingsby) M.P. for Knaresborough. Takes his family from Redhouse to Lincolnshire
Bill of Attainder against Strafford. Strafford executed	1641	Slingsby votes against it and is labelled a 'Straffordian'. Lady Slingsby, his wife, dies
Charles I comes to York, tries to take Hull. Edgehill	1642	Slingsby commands trainbands of York. Is commissioned to raise his own regiment of foot
The Queen arrives Bridlington from abroad. Siege of Hull	1643	Slingsby at Bridlington, garrisons Stamford Bridge, and takes part in siege of Hull
Scots invade England – siege of York–Marston Moor, surrender of York	1644	Slingsby in both siege and battle – afterwards marches to Lancashire and thence to Oxford via Newark
Charles I leaves Oxford, takes Leicester, is defeated at Naseby	1645	Slingsby in both engagements
Siege of Newark – Charles I surrenders to the Scots	1646	Slingsby goes to Redhouse for money during siege but returns before Newark surrenders. Goes home to Redhouse
Parliament takes Charles I from the Scots	1647	Slingsby in hiding at Redhouse
Second Civil War – siege of Colchester	1648	Slingsby corresponds with Langdale and Mayney

NATIONAL EVENTS	YEAR	FAMILY EVENTS
King Charles executed	1649	Slingsby ends his Diary
Cromwell conquers Scotland	1650	Slingsby helps a young cousin at school in York. His estates threatened with confiscation
	1651	His nephew Slingsby Bethell and the Stapyltons save the estates
Formation of the Sealed Knot	1653	John Belasyse, Slingsby's brother-in-law, the only R.C. member. Nicholas Armorer visits Slingsby at Redhouse
	1654	Slingsby delivers a letter from Charles II to Lady Fairfax. Thomas and Henry are sent abroad
Regional risings – all suppressed rule of the Major-Generals	1655	Slingsby one of the Yorkshire leaders on Marston Moor – He is captured at Redhouse
	1656	Slingsby sentenced to indefinite imprisonment in Hull Castle, where he tries to persuade garrison to surrender Hull
	1657	Cromwell orders him to be 'trepanned'
	1658	Slingsby delivers commission to Major Waterhouse – he is taken to the Tower and tried in Westminster Hall – sentenced to a traitor's death, but is executed on Tower Hill. 8th June
Cromwell dies 3 September More regional risings, which fail	1659	Thomas, now Sir Thomas, marries Fairfax meets Sir Thomas Slingsby on Marston Moor, and enters York. Monck marches on London
Charles II enters London – the Restoration	1660	

Introduction

THE STUDY OF THE ROYALIST ARMIES in the Great Civil War
has been of absorbing interest to me for more than thirty
years, and for that reason I welcome this new and
authoritative life of one of its colonels.

Sir Henry Slingsby, though he saw a good deal of active
service, fighting at Marston Moor and Naseby, as well as a
number of minor actions, was far from the typical Cavalier
of popular imagination. He was no hard-fighting *sabreur* of
the type whose leisure hours were devoted to women and
wine – what Slingsby called 'debauched Gallantry'. Goring
would have found him poor company. Reserved, independent, and pious he was a true Puritan. Convinced of the
justice of the Royalist cause, when the war was over he
refused to compound for his estates, and took part in the
abortive attempt at a rising in 1655. He became a figure of
national importance only in the last days of his life when,
trepanned by Cromwell, he was tried for 'High Treason',
and suffered for his constant loyalty.

Geoffrey Ridsdill Smith has based his biography on long
and scholarly research into seventeenth century sources,
basing much of his narrative on Sir Harry's own diary,
an invaluable authority for the period.

This is a book which throws much light on everyday
life, as well as the great events of the day. But the real test
of a book of this sort is the light it throws on the character
and motives of its chief actor. Only by understanding what
men were like in those distant days can we build up some
understanding of one of the most formative periods in
English History. After reading these pages we see Sir
Henry Slingsby as he really was, a man whose actions

sprang from Conscience, Loyalty and Honour, who by his resolute opposition to the Cromwellian usurpation played a part in paving the way for the Restoration.

PETER YOUNG

Prologue

REDHOUSE, the home of the Yorkshire cavalier Sir Harry Slingsby, lies two miles north-east of Marston Moor station and in the parish of Moor Monkton. It is approached by a winding lane which ends in a track leading down to the River Ouse, and the humble jetty by an ancient willow styled Redhouse Landing on the ordnance map. The first half mile of this lane heads straight for the White Horse of the distant Hambleton Hills, but at an old mill it forks right and thereafter wanders at will through the fields and past two or three farms till it meets Redhouse Wood and is forced to make a right-angled turn. Here, where in spring bluebells and bracken pour out from the trees to line the ditch, the visitor gets his first view of Redhouse – a gabled brick house, with tall chimneys, a steep grey roof and rows of mullion windows facing south. To the right is the 600-year-old deer park which was full of fallow deer till the first war claimed them for food; to the left a clump of sycamores on the mound where the earlier fortified manor once stood; and, alone by themselves in a field, three Scotch firs, the Jacobite signal.

Since 1902 Redhouse has been a preparatory school. In its early days when I was a boy there most visitors arrived by train and were met at the station by the school wagonette drawn by a pair of greys, sometimes also by a mounted escort of boys in Scout uniform, bearing red-and-white pennoned lances – though who was escorting whom was often in doubt. The boys' Scout patrols were named, as were the dormitories, after leaders in the Civil War; Marston Moor, where relics of the battle could still be found, was within easy riding distance; the house had its ghosts, both seen and heard; and speculation never ceased as to the whereabouts of the secret room where Slingsby hid when the soldiers were searching the house, after questioning his children of about our own age. To grow up in such an environment meant being either a little Royalist, or else a little Cromwellian.

So it came about that after four years there as a boy, a spell of sick leave as a subaltern in the first war, and six years on the staff in a number of congenial capacities after getting a history degree at Queens' College, Cambridge, where Slingsby had been a Fellow Commoner 300 years before, I felt impelled to find out more about this other Queensman whose home had become a second home to me, and whose story had never been told. In this book I have tried to tell it, letting him do so in his own words where possible.

Chapter One

1066 – 1607

ALTHOUGH HARRY SLINGSBY would still feel at home in Queens' he would be lost at Redhouse, much of which was demolished at the beginning of the nineteenth century and the remainder, with its walls refaced and leaded windows reglazed, reduced in 1860 to that 'neat' appearance which that generation admired. A century's weathering has mellowed it and ivy, climbing rose, wisteria and jasmine scaled its walls – providing what the rat-catcher, surveying the tangle with his three dogs and eight ferrets, described as a 'proper 'ighway for t'rats'. Fortunately the Jacobean chapel was considered neat enough, though the heraldic staircase was moved into it from the house, halved in width and length and with those crests, for which there was now no room, fixed here and there to the walls. Also moved from the south front of the house, and set up over the chapel doorway, was a Latin inscription in moulded brick which reads :

PRO TERMINO VITAE
SIC NOS NON NOBIS

Many people have had a go at translating it. The first line probably means, as it did in legal documents, 'for our term of life here'. The second line is an adaptation of Virgil's 'Sic Vos non Vobis' (So you not for ourselves) which he challenged the minor poet, who had done him out of an imperial reward, to complete. When he failed Virgil did it for him in four ways; so you bees make honey, you birds

I

build nests, you oxen plough, and you sheep bear wool – not for yourselves. Slingsby has challenged posterity to complete his version. If, as most think, he meant 'So we build not for ourselves' he could hardly have devised a more appropriate motto for a school.

But before this Jacobean-Victorianised Redhouse there was an earlier one, the manor house for Scagglethorpe, one of the lost villages of Yorkshire which, in Domesday Book, is called Scarchetorp and had land for three ploughs, with one villane and four bordars living on it. At the time of Edward the Confessor it had been worth ten shillings and eightpence, but at the Survey, six shillings. In the Claims two Ernuins, Ernuin Catenase and Ernuin the Priest, claimed it but the jurors prudently supported the priest.[1] By 1300 the manors of Moor Monkton and Scagglethorpe were held by the Ughtreds, who had been tenants-in-chief at the time of Domesday, and Thomas Ughtred was licensed to impark his woods and crenellate his house.[2] He fought at Crecy and was created Lord Ughtred and one of the first Knights of the Garter. Later Ughtreds were, like him, Knights of the Shire for Yorkshire, Commissioners of Array and of Oyer and Terminer, and Surveyors of 'wears, milles, stanks, stakes and kiddles in the waters of Ouse, Don, Wharf, Nidde and Derwent'.[3] They also distinguished themselves in the French and Scottish wars. Robert Ughtred who was knighted on the banks of the Somme during Suffolk's expedition in 1523, having only one daughter, sold Scagglethorpe and its manor house of Redhouse to his uncle, Sir Anthony Ughtred who was married to Elizabeth Seymour, the Queen's sister, and had at one time been interested in the foundation of Wolsey College at Oxford.[4] In 1532 he sold 'Le Rede Howse' and the park for 1000 marks to his brother-in-law Sir Edward Seymour, but with the right for himself and his wife to live there for the rest of their lives. After his death in 1534 his widow retained the right till she married Lord Cromwell. In 1560 Francis Slingsby of Scriven bought the reversion of it and 15 years later was authorised to enclose that half of Scagglethorpe Moor 'adjoining the manor house of Scagglethorpe, now commonly called the Red House'. He had married Mary

Percy, sister to the 7th and 8th Earls of Northumberland, and they had three daughters and nine sons, the eldest of whom was drowned in the Nidd while trying to rescue his servant. It was the eldest surviving son, Henry, who in 1595 'for a certain sum of money' bought 'the manor and Lordship of Skagglethorpe, alias Red Howses', and two years later the manors of Moor Monkton and Wilstrop.

He, or his father, or both, must have decided to pull down the old Redhouse and build a more spacious one some 50 yards to the south. All that now remains of the old Ughtred home are the wide moat that surrounded it, green with water plants and the waving sword leaves of the yellow flag, and its brick and stone foundations and cobbled courtyard under the grass of a rectangular mound now covered with sycamores. The light of the setting sun threads with gold the green trunks of these trees, and all day long the rooks, who took over the site, keep up their harsh but soothing chorus. A bird's eye view from one of the tree-tops, up among the nests, shows the river Ouse curling round the Ings, or meadows, to the north and beyond it the Vale of York bounded by the long blue wall of the Hambleton Hills; lying to the east is Scagglethorpe Moor with the twin towers of York Minster gleaming on the skyline; to the south the deer park and a patchwork of fields stretch away to the low ridge that overlooks Marston Moor; and west, the green rampart of Redhouse Wood leads down to the tower of Nun Monkton church and the Priory alongside which the Danes sacked on one of their upriver raids. This all-round view, apart from the present Redhouse, has hardly changed since Ughtreds surveyed it from the battlements of their manor.

The first record of the building of the new house is a contract dated 14 November 1606 between Henry (by this time Sir Henry) and two brickmakers of Woollous to dig earth in some convenient place within the Lordship of Scagglethorpe, to temper it and in three kilns burn 200,000 good and hard bricks, 12,000 good and perfect thacke tiles and 8 score ridge tiles. The first lot was to be burned before Whitsuntide, the next before Lammas and the third before Michaelmas. Sir Henry agreed to deliver at the kilns as

3

much wood and coal, sand and straw as should be necessary, to provide a horse and cart and as many wheelbarrows as were needed for loading the clay from the pit, and also to have a shed 20 yards long constructed to keep out the weather while they worked at the tiles. The cost of all the work was £40, to be paid in instalments of £5 when work began, another £5 after Christmas when they began to turn the clay and, after moulding began, 30/- a week, the residue to be paid when the work was finished. There are no contemporary plans of the new house, but a large 17th century oil painting depicts it as a Dutch-gabled, many-windowed house twice the length of the present one. The picture was painted from the deer park whence a bridge led over the fish-ponds and into the formal walled garden, with dove-cote and peach walk to the west, terrace and summer house to the east, all executed with the rigidity of the drawing board — a rigidity relieved only by undisciplined puffs of smoke from the chimneys, a flutter of white doves round the dovecote, and the deer lazing and grazing in the park. Warburton, who toured the county in 1718, has a distant pencil sketch of it in his Drawings of Gentlemen's Seats showing gables, long windows and a central turret all embowered in trees.

Our only information about the interior comes from the Diary which Harry started to write soon after he inherited the house on his father, Sir Henry's, death. He mentions the new parlour 'where the nine Muses are' (now musing as part of a screen in Knaresborough church), and above it a lodging chamber that was being painted blue and silver to match the wall hangings, bought in Bethnal Green, 'of calfe skin silvered and wrought upon with a large flower in blue worstett'. This may well have been the room, still called the King's Room, where Charles I slept in 1633 on his way to Scotland. Then there was the Star Chamber, and the Great Chamber, and the Painted Chamber. Harry added little to his father's building, 'only here and there a peice which one summer hath begun and finished,' and disapproved of the elaborate work going on at the royal palace of Theobalds, Lord Suffolk's Audley End, Lord Everie's Malton, Lord Savile's Howley and Sir Arthur

4

Ingram's Temple Newsam. 'I may see by this', he comments, 'the vanity of all worldly things which men do so much rest upon. Let a man propose to himself never so great matters, yet shall another come that may exceed him ; if he build his house like Nebuchodonoser that he may say "Is not this great Babell that I have built?" and another shall come that exceeds him, he shall think that all that is vain which he hath done or made ; we understand this in the Temple of Jerusalem which second building did exceed the first ; and in this our Archbishop aimed at in the repairing of Paul's church, to make it more glorious than before . . . I shall ever dissuade my son from effecting building, unless it be with great moderation. But whatever one doth let him resolve to please himself, for it may be it shall not please another.'

The chapel has changed little since those days. Shafts of sunlight, clear through the diamond panes or stained with the red, green and gold of the painted glass, move over the squares and triangles of the black and white marble floor, highlighting the poppy-head bench ends, the brass sconces over the choir stalls and the strapwork on the hexagonal pulpit – the only change here being that its two-sided door, if incautiously closed, is liable to trap any visiting preacher, whose entry into the pulpit is therefore closely, and hopefully, watched. 'This chapell', writes Harry, 'is built in the form of a colledge chapell ; in the east end of the chapell upon the glass is painted a Crucifix not as ordinary crucifixes are made but with a transverse peice of wood at the feet as there is for the hands ; at the feet is set the Virgin Mary, and on the one hand the picture of the Apostle St. John, and on the other Elizabeth and underneath St. Peter, St. Andrew, St. Paul. In the south window the rest of the Apostles. In the north corner is a handsome pulpit, a Table Altar-wise under the east window, with a cloath of purple colour wrought with stripes of worstett, which was my wife's own handiwork'. Sir Henry, in his household account book, notes that he has sent £13 12 0 to his brother Sir Guilford 'in a letter by Mr Perkes his boye to paie to Mr. Butler in Chancerie Lane for 9 of the Apostles for a window in the chapell at Redhowse of 3 lights 4ft high and 14in broad.' Nearly all this glass in the east and south windows was replaced by heraldic glass and allegorical figures from the Star Chamber when the house was altered, and only four apostles' amber-haloed heads remain, skied up in the top lights, with some rosy-winged cherubs for company. Among them are the arms of Lichfield whose liberal-minded Bishop Morton consecrated the chapel; and the arms of Oxford, and Cambridge where, in St. John's College hall, his portrait hangs. The three main lights now glitter with coroneted crests: the silver crescent on a crimson ground of Northumberland, the golden dragon of Cumberland, and the Prince of Wales's feathers; and below each are Slingsby coats of arms with sufficient quarterings to satisfy the most voracious student of heraldry.[5] Along the base of the window runs a commemorative inscription to the last of the Slingsbys, Sir Charles, Master of the York and Ainsty who, with his huntsman, four other men and six horses, was drowned in 1869 in the flooded Ure when the overloaded ferryboat capsized[6] – a tragedy which was headline news in the county and inspired the pamphleteers and ballad-mongers to do their worst. Sir Charles's hatchment hangs on the south wall, his coat of arms resplendent above the bold motto *Mors Janua Vitae*, Death the Gate of Life. On the opposite wall is a mural, done in river-green, of Moses and Aaron, Moses pointing with his rod to the ten commandments and looking, as one visitor remarked, like an elderly billiard marker. Over the open screen that divides the chancel from the ante-chapel is a gallery, approached by the heraldic staircase, whence one can examine in greater comfort the detail of the great east window that soars up in columns of light from the shade of the sanctuary. Daily services are still said in the words of that prayer book, 'very well seasoned and crumbed with the Bread of Life', which Sir Henry's chaplain used 300 years before.[7] Seasoned too with the bread of country life, as befits a chapel set in such rural seclusion where the word may have been less intelligible to some of the congregation than the birdsong and garden scents and sounds of the beasts in the fields that

6

drifted in through the open windows on summer evenings, or the force of the tree-felling gales that on winter nights hammered on the massive door till the candles guttered and smoked.

1 Y.A.J. XXXVI, 280, 310.
2 Confirmation of Gifts, Ed III, 1334, 1342.
3 Pat. Rolls Ed III, 1353.
4 B.M. Add MS, 24, 965 f. 197 b, 207.
5 Much of this glass was almost certainly the work of Bernard Dirickhoff who also painted the Fairfax glass in Gilling Castle. Recent examination of the window preparatory to restoration has revealed that the top lights and stone headings are 14th century, taken almost certainly from Nun Monkton Priory, in ruins after the Dissolution.
6 One relic is a silver statuette of Sir Charles's horse, Saltfish, which caused the accident by jumping overboard, pulling Sir Charles after him. The horse got caught up in the chains but Sir Charles swam towards the far bank. When Saltfish had freed himself he followed his master like a dog, but by the time he reached him it was too late. Saltfish eventually clambered out further downstream.
   One of the survivors was Sir George Wombwell of Newburgh Priory, which his grandfather, who married a daughter of the last Earl Fauconberg, had inherited. As Cardigan's A.D.C. he had also survived the charge of the Light Brigade, relics of which are on view at Newburgh today.
7 Archbishop Toby Matthews' Register: '20 May 1627. Matthew Stanton M.A. Queens' College, Cambridge. Ludimagister in domu Henrici Slingsby militis. Ordained priest.'

Chapter Two

1580 – 1621

SIR HENRY, the builder of Redhouse, had two brothers who will figure in this tale – Guilford, who became Comptroller of the Navy, and William who served with Guilford in the successful expedition against Cadiz in 1596 as Commissary of the Fleet, and 'the syckest of syx hundred in our ship' as he told his father in a letter written after they had ridden out a storm. Henry had his own troubles, but in another sort of fleet, the Fleet prison where, while trying to release his father he was himself committed for debt 'after being enforced to go in secret corners, not daring to come abroad to follow my busyness.' After his father's death in 1600 he was involved in a number of suits in the Duchy Court of Lancaster which he lost, together with certain offices he had held. But this did not prevent him from representing the Borough of Knaresborough in parliament, together with William, in 1601. Nor from visiting Ireland the next year as one of the 'undertakers' for colonising lands taken from the Earl of Desmond. He had been granted 8,000 acres in Tipperary and on this visit he was knighted in Dublin Castle by Lord Mountjoy.[1]

Some time before this he had married Frances Vavasour, a papist, and they had fourteen children of whom Harry was number nine, with one elder brother and seven elder sisters. It is in his letters that he reveals himself chiefly to us so it is worthwhile noticing two which are quite different from the moralising ones he wrote to his children. Both were written when he was already the father of eight,

8

to an unidentified lady, not his wife, whom he calls 'Cousin'. 'How much I am beholden to you for your love yourself best knows,' he writes, 'and how much I think myself beholding to you I am enforced to reveal, because I have not sufficient means as I would to manifest a requital. The distance of our dwelling is so injurious to our desires, as I neither list utter what I conceive nor urge what I desire, though I make no doubt but love though unwillingly will grant anything. But I should happily and not unworthily purchase blame if I should kindle that which of itself is almost ready to flame and not to be at hand to tend the fire.' And a month later 'What effecting power your letter hath I very well know for since my many times reading of it I have found a great alteration in myself, sometimes over-joyed in seeing your affection assured me, and then again I hold myself much wronged, yet I cannot [permit] any to be my love who I judge to be too much void of commiseration in not affording us that comfort which other lovers enjoy.' None of her letters to him, no others of his to her, survive so their secret is their own.

In the meantime his family continued to increase. But their mother, Frances, remains a shadowy figure in the background. Only one of her letters is extant, written from Redhouse in 1610 to her husband in London about their eldest son, William's, imminent journey to France with a tutor. 'At Martinmas,' she writes, 'I was verie sicke and since have had bad health, and have taken a long leave of our Sonne excepte physique helpe, which by God's grace I meane to try the nexte weeke. If I live I hope to be a partaker of your comfort at his retourne, and if I die I must leave to you him and all the reste of our children beseeching God to make you a loving father and send you health and long life amongst them.

She died the next year. One cannot help wondering whether she ever read her husband's 'Instructions for Mr Snell for the guiding of his pupil Willm. Slingesbye', and if so what she thought of them. They begin with 'the principles of religion' – daily prayers, attending services of the reformed church, grace at meals, bible reading and keeping the sabbath holy – followed by instructions for 'scholer learning and Frenche. That nexte unto religion he first applye his latin that he may have some sence of the congruitie thereof and maye a little understande ordinary thinges when he shall reade them in latin whilst Frenche is wantinge.' The tutor must speak to him only in Latin or French unless he has 'occasion to give him some holesome precepte which cannot be understood by him but in English.' When he could understand enough French he might 'goe to papist's sermons when he cannot have the meanes to goe to the protestant's; and when he shall have competent language he doe not soe much as meditate anything to himself but in ffrench. Of this he will finde greate use and profitt.' Mathematics are dismissed in one line. But 'for healthe he is to walke and take the aire often so that all his learninge be not sitting but somtymes walkinge, and by way of familiar discourseing will be less wearisome and happilye more profitable. That somtymes he take some cooling posset to keep his blood and liver in good temper; that he take heed of fruites and especially grapes for they breed the bloody fluxes and are very dangerous for young persons; that he temper well his wyne with water; that he take heed what companie he keep in too familiar a fashion for the ffrenche are of an ill conversacion and full of many loathesome diseases; the Dutch have a falte worse than that, both for soule, bodye, thrifte and reputation.' On this enigmatic note the health instructions end. In a separate paragraph, under 'Extraordinarie Learninge,' William is to 'applye well his writinge, learne his weapon, learne to dance, learne to ride.' In addition he had to keep a journal of his travels, a copy of which was to be sent once a quarter to his father. In it were to be listed the towns and villages he passed through, their churches, castles and rulers; their parliaments, universities and the trade they did with each other and with England; the names of all merchants he dealt with; details of the posts and messengers he used, and descriptions of 'the townes' streets and their distinct habitations that his directions being soe made maye be playne to everbodyes' understandinge.' He must account for all his expenses and make a duplicate copy of the journal; and 'once every 14 dayes read over these Articles.' One's sympathies go with the boy, even more perhaps with the tutor.

Harry had been sent three years before, when he was only six, to be boarded and taught by the vicar of Foston, near York, the Reverend Phatuel Otby, and here he was joined by his younger brother, Thomas. Their father, still pre-occupied with law suits in London, was also High Sheriff of the county. One of these lawsuits caused him to miss the 1611 Summer Assize in York and be fined £200, which would have been heavier still if a certain Baron Snigge had not, for a ten-pound tip, used his influence with the Ex-chequer. The Reverend Phatuel, in loco parentis at Foston, continued his task of educating the Slingsby boys, with a strong emphasis on Latin, (Harry's 'Linguae Latinae Exercitatio' with his name on it, still exists). He was the last resident vicar of Foston till Lady Holland procured the living for Sidney Smith who, of his first sermon there as incumbent, wrote, 'When I began to thump the cushion of my pulpit, as is my wont when preaching, the accumu-lated dust of 150 years made such a cloud that for some minutes I lost sight of my congregation.' It was perhaps a pity that Harry, a serious-minded boy, did not learn to laugh with this 'Smith of Smiths.'² The letter he wrote from Foston in December 1612 to brother William 'a l'Academie pres le porte St. Honoree a Paris', was a curious though, in the light of later events, revealing Christmas letter for an eleven-year-old to have composed. It starts with a line in Latin :
'Expertus in multis, in magnis, in bonis'
and continues, 'This posie (most lovinge and beloved brother) which I have placed as I may say "in frontispicio literarum" is not sett down for a theeme to be declared of but as a memorandum which I meane (God willinge) to sett before me, as it were a continuall marke to aime at in all my actions through the whole of my life. For this only shall be my endeavour to gaine and gett knowledge and experience everie day, and that not in any particular Art or science but in so many as I may, and these not of small weight or little moment but both the greatest and the best I may learne, God Almightie my heavenlie father assisting me with his

11

(. . .) and our deere and naturell father with maintenance, and my careful Tutors and diligent maysters with instruction. Thus sending you the taiste of my hartie desire and the vew of my stedfast resolution, I take my leave, giveing you hartie thankes for your discourse which you sent us, and praieing continuallie for your good healthe and happie retorne into England.'

The wished-for happy return took place the next year, thanks mostly to a letter Sir Henry received from Mr Snell, almost demented by this time one would imagine from trying to carry out his employer's Instructions, suggesting that William's interests should be stimulated by travel further afield, and with another tutor. His suggestion had dire consequences. William came home and preparations were begun for a journey to Italy. The account book shows purchases of a felt hat 'with feather with a touch of murrey in it', white shoes, a silver seal engraved with the Slingsby coat of arms, a book called 'The Italian Scholmaister', a perfumed satin bag embroidered 'with silke and gold and lynned with taffatie' and containing a comb case lined with green velvet, and a glass, brush and combs. A 'black nagge' was bought for him in Smithfield and a 'grissel nagge' for his man. He carried with him a letter of credit for £50 to be presented to a Mr Burlomatique in Florence. Here the records end, and all that is known is that four years later he was killed in Florence.

One year after this tragedy, 1618, Harry, now sixteen, went up to Queens' College, Cambridge, and the letters that passed between him and his father from February 1618 till July 1621 tell us a lot about each of them. Harry's first letter concerns his Fellow Commoner's gown, an elaborate affair of 'Turkey grogroune, because no stuff will do better in black than that', gold lace, velvet, baize and buttons, and he sends a list from his tailor of all that is needed. Sir Henry, though observing that it 'arises to a greate deale of monie', promises to send the materials but warns Harry to wear his new gown only when going to church or the Schools. 'Bid your taylor make it long enough', he adds, 'for you have yett a year or towe to grow in. But you must remember this difference of garment for Fellow Commoners is not for their

Redhouse in the 17th century. The door in the peach walk where Slingsby was captured is hidden by the dovecote in the bottom left hand corner. Only the west, or left hand, half of the house now remains.

(by permission of the Borough of Harrogate Public Library)

The pulpit and altar rails in Redhouse Chapel.   *Photograph by G. Bernard Wood*

own meritt but for the dignitie of the Fellows into whose societie they are admitted.' The new suit to go with his new gown which Harry had asked for, spicing his request with a bit of Latin, was refused and in a postscript he was advised 'to sett aside for a while the pleasures of apparel' and get down to work.

The problem of rooms, which faces all men up at university, was a problem then. 'I do as yet keep my old chamber,' writes Harry 'and also my chamber fellow, Mr Fines, nor doth know untill we know certainly of the young Earl of Lincoln's coming how we shall be lodged, but peradventure you know concerning that matter better than we. If my Lord do not come up I think I shall keep where I do; if he do I know not what will be donne.' Sir Henry urges Harry not to change his room, 'for it is a very fair one and stands very convenientlie', even though the Earl 'is resolved to spend some more tyme at Cambridge.' He is glad of this, 'for if his course be sober and religious all the rest maie blush if they do not imitate him and follow the course of so worthy a leader.' For the next two years all was well but then, in the tutor's absence, some 'harsh work' was done by a Mr Roberts which threatened the loss of both room and bedfellow. 'Care the less so you hold your chamber', writes the father reassuringly, 'for though the beddesteade may be his I am sure the bed is your own and you maie in reasonable tyme get a beddesteade.' This domestic problem remains, for the reader, unsolved.

Harry was expected to write to his seven sisters, 'some one weeke and some another.' This was asking too much. Anne, his senior by eight years, writes pathetically, 'If you would have taken paine to a remembered mee with one letter I should have taken paine, tho it be a paine, to have answered it, that in this time of our absence our minds might have intermooved by letters when I consider of our long absence, and that their hath been so little remembrance one of another.' He was also expected to write to his old schoolmaster, Phatuel Otby, 'and when you do wryghte, wryghte so as he maie well perceave you have learned to wryghte' – and to write better, one hopes, than did Phatuel himself whose writing is a rare example of illegible flourishes.

'Do not at any tyme accustom yourself to a ragged hand',
continues Sir Henry. 'I do speak thus much because of
your uppermost superscription which made me allmost
blush to see it. If you do not look well to it your brother will
go before you. P.S. Your letters seem to be before the
Conquest, for they are without date for the most parte.'

Harry's next gaffe was to enclose in his letter another
letter, 'but God knows to whom' replies his father, 'and
therefore I send it back to you that you maie direct it. I
cannot but think that Sir Archer's hand is in your letters'
(Archer was an older friend). 'No man loves to be deceived
but in this case I should be most glad to be mistaken. P.S.
You have many nephews, but whom you meane here I know
not excepte your pollecie be that this letter without superscription shoulde serve them all, for it is alike to all'. As
Harry had already more than twenty nephews his policy, if
it was one, seems sound enough. However he returned the
letter, this time addressed, apologised for his negligence and
expressed grief and surprise to learn that his father was 'so
incredulous as not to believe my letter to be of my own
enditing, when I myself am most sure that it was. But you
need not doubt it, for of all manner of stiles I can best
conceive of golden eloquence, and it is that which can
sharpen the dullest wits (if it please you you maie "peri-
culum facere")', in other words try it yourself. Thus off to
a good start he continues, 'Sir Archer told me it was your
pleasure, if I thought it fitting, to ride the Greate Horse
again. Therefore I determine (my boldness being grounded
upon the assurance of your favour) to beginne upon Munday
being the 20th of September, Mr Paine being desirous,
he having noe scholers and allsoe having gotte a new
Horse.' Sir Henry's comments are not extant.

Only once did Harry take the initiative in this epistolary
duel, beginning: 'Sir, Diogenes being asked wherefore he
ate his dinner on the highway, he answered because he was
an hungered on the highway; therefore if you should ask
me why and wherefore I may get worse at one time than
at another I answer because I am in more haist at one time
than at another.' It was this very haste which annoyed his
father. 'I sent you some violl strings last weeke', he writes,

'but whether you receaved them or noe you make noe mention; I send you this weeke your foils which Mr Dobson sent me yesterday to my lodging.' A year later he was still complaining 'That you receaved anie letters or anie shirtes from me you write nothing. I have admonished you heretofore that when you receave anie thinges you should at least take knowledge of the receipte though it be not worthie thanks; and if it be worthie thankes you ought to remember that allsoe, as in this case of sending your shirtes without being putt in minde from you . . . Besides I have putt you in minde formerly that when you answeare anie letters you should laie before you the letters you had receaved and to everie pointe thereof make some answer. But of letters I wrote by the last carrier concerning manie pointes I have noe answeare at all. Such instructions as I shall give you ought to be regarded, especially not being ill because they come from me.'

The carrier was, of course Hobson, of 'Hobson's Choice' notoriety, and Harry once protested that he had not acknowledged some maps his father had sent him because he had missed the post. But this did not work. 'I maie make excuse of haist,' replies his father, 'because the carrier staies but one night in London and lies so farr from me. But you cannot, the carrier staying three daies in Cambridge . . . But if he takes too much leisure in delivering my letters chide him for it, for I paie him sufficientlie.' Harry did so, but was no match for Hobson, who as he reports, 'did so peremptorily answer me that I had like to have spent my time and lost my labor.' He was lucky perhaps to have lost nothing more. Sir Henry replies, 'I intende to provide you with a mappe of Asia but to avoide the like quarrel with your carrier, and save 4d of carriage, I will bring it myself, for after the tearme I shall have some occasion to come to Newmarket and then I will not balke Cambridge.'

Some reports of Harry's state of mind must have reached his father who now wrote, 'Be most assured of my love, which you maie be sure to have if you will, and can hardlie recover if you once lose it, which makes me more concerned to give you this pre-warning. Some tell me that you are sadde and melancholly. It is much against my will that you shoulde be soe and my desire is you shoulde have all fitting recreation that you be as merrie as you like in honest and civill compaynie. And if your Tutor be a little too reserved in granting you tymes of recreation, since I will not be contented that you shallowlie [to the ill example of others] take it at your owne hand, soe I will, upon your just complaynte, enjoyne him to amende it. Soe maie you have your desire but not your will. Marke well my wordes and laie them up in your harte. Vale!'

But the Tutor also received a rap. 'I must confess I was not a little disconcerted,' writes Sir Henry, 'with my sonne going to London contrarie to my directions, and altho he did wryghte to me it was by your consent, yett I was not satisfied because I herde it not from you.' But John Preston was a most exceptional tutor. Even Sir Henry, who never wasted words of praise, had told Harry in a postscript 'By the multitude of your Tutor's pupils you maie well perceave their is some matter of worth in him.' Fuller says 'he was the greatest pupil-monger in England, having sixteen fellow-commoners (most heirs to fair estates) admitted in one year to Queens' College, and provided convenient accommodation for them'.[3] Among those with Harry were the Yelvertons, sons of the puritan Sir Henry Yelverton, the 4th Earl of Lincoln, two sons of Sir Arthur Capel, and their cousin Arthur, later Lord, Capel. Preston was moreover the most popular preacher in Cambridge and whenever he preached in Queens' members of other colleges had to be excluded.

It was no sad and melancholy Harry however who two years later admitted that whereas he had previously neglected his work and the 'Acts in Towne' for matters of less moment but of more consequence to himself he now, with greater maturity of judgement 'findes the sweetness of them and begins to frequent them' – a practice not unknown to undergraduates today as their finals approach. The Acts he refers to were the Disputations held in the Schools and Great St. Mary's church, attended by two-year men as observers, thence rising in their fourth year to be 'questionists' and to qualify, if successful, as Bachelors. Harry, as son and heir of a knight, was allowed with other Fellow Commoner sons of peers, to attend those held in Great St. Mary's when royalty was present. Of an assembly of clergy in the church he writes 'Mr Wincope did very well and with great applause, and soe every day one Act or another', continuing in Latin to ask who could live more happily than he now does and what could be more desirable than this life he leads. John Preston took a prominent part in these Disputations, and once delighted James I, a keen hunting man, with his skill when the debate was on the theme of whether dogs could make syllogisms. His lively divinity lectures were crowded out and Sir Henry, who often asked Harry, without getting any answer, about his preparation for the holy communion – 'I praie you to think seriously of it, and remember that you come to feaste with the greate God of Heaven, and lett your thoughts and conversation be answerable to soe precious a banquett' – was finally content to leave this to Preston.

Harry's musical education he viewed with less enthusiasm. Of some viol strings he had sent he writes, 'You had need to plaie the good husband with them and keep them charelie for they cost me five shillings', and he tells Harry to ask his uncle to help him to buy a good viol and to recommend a teacher. 'Whether you have anie practice in singing of partes,' he continues, 'I heare nothinge, but would not have you forgett it, for it was the onlie qualitie you had did moste commend you. I must confess there be other thinges more woorthie than itt, yett having it were a shame to forgett it through a little idle negligence. Cease not till you gett Mr Richard's songes pricked in your booke for I am not well pleased they are soe long adoing. P.S. Use your swinge and take care to goe upright.'

But Harry was not Sir Henry's only parental concern. Thomas, his younger son, was now at a school in France after leaving Foston, and two of the unmarried daughters were living with relations, and apparently on short allowances. For 16-year-old Eleanor writes, 'Loving Father, I intreate you to send mee some money against New Yeare's tide for I shall stand in great need; and after that you will be pleased to send mee 4 paires of silk garters to bestow upon my Lord's grandchildren, and one paire of bracelets and some two pair of little gloves for the other children.' This was followed by a demand from Sir Thomas Ingram who was looking after another daughter: 'Her allowance is so small as she cannot maintain herself in clothes as is necessary for her, considering she ought to sett herself out as much to her advantage as she may to inamour the young men that may look upon her, which may perhaps gett her so good a husband as may save you £1000 in her portion. In earnest you needs must allow her more. Pray let me heare effectually from you by this bearer.'

To add to these money worries someone must have told Harry that he was a fool to be wasting his time at Cambridge, for Sir Henry writes 'If any one goes about to persuade you that the scoole is not a fitt place for you do not beleeve it, for when I come to London I intend three tymes a weeke to dyne with you, and I am sure the place is good and no disparagement if you spende your tyme well.' He goes on to remind Harry of a visit he must pay to Lady Calvert when he is next in London, and how he is to conduct it. 'When Mr. Secretary [her husband] comes home remember to present your service to him; you must allsoe be mindful that he is a privie councillor and therefore in your speeches to him you must use these wordes "Your Honour", for all privie councillors, tho but Knights, are still honourable.'[4]

Through the spring and summer of 1621 the correspondence is mostly about whether Harry should stay up for a fourth year or go abroad, if he could find 'a fitt man for the journey' who must be religious, discreet and frugal. Harry at first was inclined to stay up, which his father approved of though leaving the final decision to him – 'So long as you ground your desires upon reason you maie draw me which way you will, for it is your good I hunt after.' Then it was that Preston proposed, as his biographer, Thomas Ball, writes, to take one of his pupils abroad with him, 'a Yorkshire gentleman, Sir Henry Slingesby his son and heyre, and did accordingly acquaint his father and make provision for it long before.'[5] Harry jumped at this offer and wrote, 'My Tutor doth fully intende to goe, and soe do I (since it hath pleased you to lett me goe) even "flagrare desiderio" in consideration how usefull a journey it will be and profitable. Only he would intreate you to be very private in procuring a licence lest any know. I shall be ready against Wensday after the Commencement at such time as you shall send.' The Commencement was the 2nd of July when degrees were granted.

For some time Preston had been planning a journey to the Netherlands in order to improve his Latin with a view to obtaining the Lady Margaret Professorship of Divinity then vacant, and had already procured a licence for himself 'with all the secrecy that could be a great while before he meant to use it, that he might conceale it from the College and University. But this secrecy begat suspicion that there was some plot and it was resented the more because no clergyman was made acquainted with it. The opinion was that something was brewing against the Episcopacy. This they were sure of, that Amsterdam was in the Netherlands, and ever bin fatall to the Hierarchy.'[6]

In August Preston left Cambridge, telling everyone in College that he was going to spend the summer vacation with his friend Sir Richard Sandes at Throwley in Kent, and 'drinke, if he saw cause, of ye Turnebridge Waters.' Here Harry joined him, to await the arrival of his licence. Sir Richard's eldest son, George, was only a few months older than Harry and, though war and personal tragedy were to engulf them both, life was still unclouded for these young men as they rode through the Throwley woods or along the downs with views out to sea where adventure beckoned. At last two letters arrived from Sir Henry, a long one for Preston (not extant) and a shorter one for Harry which read : 'There is a prettie fine pink will be at Gravesend on Tuesday nighte to goe to Flushing. I will send you thither a passe from the Archduke's Embassador to goe from the Hague to Antwerp . . . I find by examination that it is from Calais to Brussels 120 English miles, too long a waie to travell in these troubless tymes without a passe, and there-fore my resolution is that you shall come back to Gravesend and goe with the pink, or else staie and not goe at all. I will be short because you maie see what I have written in my letter to Mr Preston. This advise of getting a passe from the Archduke's Embassador I mett withall this daie at the Exchange and might ere this have mett with somewhat else as needful as that had not Mr Preston's haste and unnecessarie secrecy hindered it.'

Sir Henry may have intended to be short but he could not resist the usual lecture. 'I will now a little tell you of your errours. I finde your violl booke which is of more value than any printed booke, and some other bookes of yours together with your clothes, hatt, spurrs and other necessaries left at random, presuming belike that eyther your father must take the paine and care to put them in safety or else leave them to the wide world to be lost never to see them more. Whether such negligence as this be greatly to be condemned or no I refer it to yourself. But I tell you this, not as an essential faulte for which I would chide you, but as an errour which stands in neede of reformation. For we are taught by the spirit of God to be "prudentes ut serpentes et innocentes ut columbae".[7] You are a little eyther by nature or custom too sluggish, and too heedless of thinges that concern you. Watchfulness, care and diligence are the waies that bring us to perfection and no good thing can be attained without labour. And soe I hope by the fruits of your travell to see the reformation of these your errours.'

He might have been more doubtful about the fruits had he seen Preston boarding the boat attired, not as reverend Tutor, but 'in the garb and notion of a gentleman, with his scarlet cloake, gold hat band and all things answerable.'[8] And his doubts would have doubled had he known that the Lord Keeper had detailed a spy to follow the movements of tutor and pupil 'and to observe and give intelligence once weekly of all that passed.'[9] The cause of all Preston's secrecy was that, briefed by Buckingham, he was now charged with a delicate political mission. The Thirty Years War had just started and the protestant King and Queen of Bohemia, Frederick the Elector Palatine and Elizabeth, James I's daughter, had been driven from their kingdom by the Emperor and from the Palatinate by the Spaniards. For dynastic reasons, though against the will of the country, James was anxious to marry Prince Charles to the Spanish

Infanta and hoped that this marriage might effect the restoration of the Palatinate to his son-in-law, since he could not afford to help him with an army in the field. Then came a desperate letter from Elizabeth to Buckingham, imploring him to persuade her father to send 'some effectual comfortable answeare that may ease his [her husband's] melancholie, for I confess it troubles me to see him soe. I pray lett none know this but His Majesty and my Brother.'[10] This letter quite possibly precipitated Preston's journey, which had a double purpose. First he was to reassure Frederick that there would be no Spanish match till the Palatinate had been restored; and secondly he was to sound other courts, catholic as well as protestant, as to Spain's real attitude towards the marriage and the restoration of the Palatinate and report back to Buckingham.

Preston and his pupil went to The Hague where Elizabeth was with two of her children, her eldest son and little Rupert, then nearly two. The Queen was much taken with Preston and tried to persuade him to stay as her chaplain. On the second part of his mission Preston gave out that he was 'a Protestant gentleman that was willing to finde out the truth, and accordingly was courted by them very much and solicited to be a Papist.' The truth he was really after turned out to be unpalatable – that Spain would not, or could not, do what James wanted.

The two travellers returned to England. Preston made his report to Buckingham and arrived at Queens' punctually in time for the Michaelmas term and, scorning all rumours circulating among his colleagues that 'he had bin beyond the seas, showed them that it was incredible, and woundered at their sillyness, that they would believe so unlikely a relation. The matter was not great now all was past, and so it rested doubtfull and undetermined.' Beards must have fairly wagged in hall then.

What was less doubtful was Preston's promotion, the reward perhaps promised by Buckingham, who now wrote to the old Master[11] of puritan Emmanuel College offering generous provision for him if he would resign in favour of Preston. This he eventually did – and lived to be 103 – and Preston was, after much lobbying and shady manoeuvring, elected to the Mastership the next year, 1622, and escorted to his new college in triumphant procession by members of Queens'. His early death six years later, at the age of 40, at least spared him the anguish of seeing some of his pupils on opposite sides in the Civil War. The portrait of Elizabeth of Bohemia, which now hangs in the President's Lodge at Queens', may have been one of his bequests to the college.

Harry, finished with Cambridge, returned to Redhouse, now able, one hopes, to meet his father on more equal terms. But the correspondence that had passed between them suggests this would not have been easy. His father's disapproving eye spotted all his weaknesses and none of his virtues. He had no mother to confide in, all but one of his sisters were married, and his elder favourite brother was dead. Sad and silent are two of the words used to describe him, but we know that under this reserve was developing a courageous independence of judgment which was to surprise some of his friends.

1   Calvert, 'History of Knaresborough', 370.
2   Hesketh Pearson, 'The Smith of Smiths'.
3   Thomas Fuller, D.D., 'The History of the Worthies of England'.
4   Sir George Calvert, Secretary of State 1619–24, created Baron Baltimore in 1625; planted colonies in Newfoundland and Maryland. J. J. Cartwright, 'Chapters of Yorkshire History', 199–200.
5   ' "The Life of the Renowned Dr. Preston", writ by his pupil Thomas Ball, D.D., minister of Northampton in the year 1628,' 75.
6   Ball, 73. Fuller says Preston 'was a perfect politician, and used (lapwing-like) to flutter on that place which was furthest from his eggs'.
7   'Wise as serpents and harmless as doves' (Matthew, X, 16) This may have been a favourite text of Sir Henry's for it is inscribed beside the two-headed figure, with serpents twined round the right arm, which is now in the chapel east window. Below it is James I's motto, Beati pacifici.
8   Ball, 75.
9   Ball, 74. The Lord Keeper was Bishop Williams.
10 Irvonwy Morgan, 'Prince Charles's Puritan Chaplains', 87. M. A. E. Green, 'Elizabeth, Queen of Bohemia', 422.
11 Laurence Chaderton.

Chapter Three

1621 – 1634

THE YEAR AFTER HARRY went down from Cambridge his youngest sister, Eleanor, who had written so appealingly for pocket money, was married to Sir Arthur Ingram whose father, Sir Arthur, was one of the richest men in England and a notorious social climber. He had just bought Temple Newsam for £12,000 and begun to rebuild it on a palatial scale. The only room of the original house left untouched was that in which Darnley, James I's father, had been born. Sir Arthur's wealth came from various sources – monopolies, control of the Port of London, sale of crown lands, titles and tavern licences, and other judicious and lucky speculations. Almost everything he touched turned to gold. The life-size portrait of this 'self-righteous crook',[1] as his biographer calls him, hangs at the foot of the great staircase at Temple Newsam whence his eyes coldly follow the crowds who visit his mansion, stare up at the text in great letters of gold round the parapet which begin with the Gloria and end with 'Health and Plenty within this House', and refresh themselves in the cafetaria set up in the stables. To this palace Arthur and Eleanor came to live, for 'Old Arthur' had built for himself a luxurious Italianate house in York surrounded by exotic gardens, a bowling green, tennis court and covered fish tanks. To consolidate his establishment in society he was building a hunting lodge at Sheriff Hutton for the entertainment of royal and noble guests. Harry's father could not, even if he wished to, compete with such ostentation at Eleanor's wedding in the little parish

23

church of Moor Monkton with its two small bells given by his great-grandfather, the 5th Earl of Northumberland.

Eleanor was the last of the sisters to be married. Elizabeth, the eldest, had been married in Knaresborough in 1604 to Sir Thomas Metcalfe of Nappa Hall. Legends of this Thomas, nicknamed 'The Black Knight', and his escort of three hundred Metcalfes all mounted on Yorkshire Greys when he was Chancellor of the Duchy of Lancaster, of his private wars (for which he was fined £2000 in the Star Chamber but never paid up), and of his 'roystering hospitality and reckless extravagance' which finally ruined him, still linger in Wensleydale.[2] It was perhaps to recoup the family fortunes that the Metcalfes lived at Redhouse for some years. A servant of Lady Metcalfe's died here from a surfeit of plums and a chill caught by sitting on the grass by the ferryside. As he lay dying he talked ceaselessly of his own home and how he longed to be there, 'Tho' I do think,' Harry wrote in the Diary, 'he lay better here than if he were at his own home. And yet we never talk of nor desire heaven, tho' it be our best home' – a theme he returned to when he himself faced certain death.

The second sister, Mary, married Sir Walter Bethell, Surveyor of the East Riding to James I and a puritan, and went to live at Alne, six miles from Redhouse, where Anne, who never married, often used to stay. The vicar of Alne 'Tought the word so weakly' writes Anne to her father, 'that one can find no prophet nor comfort in it', and she spent more than a year trying to persuade the Bethells to find another man, and herself explored the neighbourhood in search. This started a host of rumours which reached her father's ears and caused him to tax her with the lot – what did she do when she went to York, where did she stay and why, how did she receive the communion, what had the preacher, just out of prison in York, said to her in the garden at Alne while the Bethells and their other guests talked in the parlour after Sunday dinner about 'bees and beasts and kine?' Sir Henry was, with some reason, fearful of the effects of extreme puritanism and especially popular preachers on this girl who said that she took no 'comfort in the plesurs of this world, but my delite is to spend my dais here that

24

hereafter I may live for ever.' It is refreshing to read, in one of her later letters, that she contemplated riding with her man-servant to Bath, which was once more becoming the fashionable spa it had been in Roman times, instead of taking the waters nearer home at Harrogate, 'The English Spaw' discovered in 1571 by her great-uncle William Slingsby.[3] From another of her letters we learn that the joiner who was making the pulpit for Redhouse chapel had died, leaving it unfinished in his shop, and that she had arranged with his widow to hire two men to finish it. Let us hope that in due course she heard some good sermons from it.

Sir Henry, a pillar of the Church of England, was as opposed to catholicism as he was to puritanism and tried to convert a 'cousin', Lady Jane Englefield, from her romanism. His letters are not extant but she, in her first reply, writes[4] 'I wonder much that so wise a man as your self would present unto me such a kind of letter', and then proceeds to demolish it point by point. In her second she expresses surprise that he is still unconvinced and concludes, tongue in cheek, that he must be 'in penurie of friendly divines that you seeke resolution of controversies from me, sillie woman.' Nevertheless he may well have felt a need to resolve these controversies, faced as he was, and was to be, with sons and daughters-in-law of varying shades of belief.

Katherine, the third sister, married Sir John Fenwick. They lived in Wallington Hall and became noted for their hospitality on both sides of the Border. Fenwick sat in parliament as one of the members for Northumberland and, as Charles I's Master of the Royal Studs, gave him 'the swiftest horse in England'.[5] He was said to be 'the greatest horsemaster for running horses that ever was in Christendom.'[6]

Alice, the fourth sister, was married in Moor Monkton church to Thomas Waterton of Walton Hall, near Wakefield, a fortified house surrounded by a lake and approached by a drawbridge. The Watertons were Roman Catholics and one of the leaders of Gunpowder Plot, three years after this marriage, was Thomas's cousin, Thomas Percy, who had hired the house, adjacent to the Houses of Parliament, in which to store the powder. Sir Henry was involved, with Northumberland's officers, in the investigations after the plot and actually talked to Percy at supper in Wetherby before there was any documentary, though plenty of hearsay, evidence against him.[7] A few days later he was killed resisting arrest at a house in Holbeach where he and other conspirators had taken refuge. In the meantime Northumberland, strongly, though wrongly, suspected of being in the know since Percy was his cousin and had visited him the day before 'the villainy should have been enacted', had been placed under house arrest with the Archbishop of Canterbury and was later committed to the Tower. Both incidents would have touched the Slingsbys closely, related as they were to the two men.

The fifth sister, Frances, married Brian Stapylton of Myton-on-Swale nine miles upriver from Redhouse. Brian was Receiver General of the North for Charles I. Two of his sons will figure later in this tale, and his two nephews, Robert and Philip, had been up at Queens' with Harry. Philip, known as 'the Presbyterian' there, already showed some of the fire that was later to make him famous.

It was now Harry's turn in the marriage market and Sir George Goring, later the Earl of Norwich, wrote to his friend Sir Arthur Ingram :[8] 'By this time I suppose young Mr Slingsby hath seen my eldest daughter, which makes me send these few lines to you desiring you to try with all conveniency what hopes of liking between them there may be, that accordingly we may either proceed cheerfully or stop without further hopes of second motions. I confess myself ingeniously to you, as to my well-known friend, that I should infinitely joy in this matter because of their dispositions which would sort so well, and that not only they, but we also, their parents, would reap the comfort of such concurrence. Did I not hear of the young gentleman as I do I could well hold my peace and tack about some other way. But I not only desire his alliance but his contentment also in the best degree, by fitting him with such a one as may not have her mind and her body in two several places, which I see too usual these days. Did I know her unhealthy I would not throw away my money to abuse her. I will assure you that above these three years she never had a touch of her former distemper and then it was but for a short time. £2000 I shall roundly pay with her, and as for other things wherein my credit with my friends may serve that worthy gentleman Sir Henry Slingsby, assure them that I should more readily assist them than they can call me to them, and I hope let them see more clearly that I have no other end in this wish of my eldest daughter first than to pay her her birthright and suit their humours so as we may all joy the more after.' Up till now Sir George had been as successful in his business dealings as Old Arthur, but in this project both failed. Whether the slightly patronising tone of the letter was conveyed, however inadvertently, by Ingram ; or whether the girl's health alarmed Sir Henry ; or whether Harry's own views prevailed, we shall never know.

Instead she married William, Lord Brereton, of Ireland. When, four years later, Harry married Barbara Belasyse, daughter of the first Viscount Fauconberg of Newburgh Priory, he acquired in John Belasyse, a brother-in-law who was to be as distinguished a soldier as George Goring became. Harry and Barbara were married in Kensington church, and lived in London at first. There is an entry in Sir Henry's account book of thirty six shillings paid to Harry 'for the increase of his allowance of diett for 3 weekes at Christmas over and above his weeklie allowance for himselfe and his wife at six shillings a peece.' Soon after the wedding Barbara wrote to her father to thank him for giving her 'to so good a husband, whose condition is so good and loving to mee as I assure myselfe we shall neither of us have cause to repente.'

But the business side of the marriage was not so harmonious. A year and a half later Sir Henry writes to his son, at great length and in much the old vein : 'You have been so indisposed to follow my councells as I know not what to saie ; yett lett me put you in minde of what hath passed between us, that you maie see your own errour, for if I doe not pittie it, that have but little cause (you having resisted me in a trifle and neglected me in my councells) I knowe not whoe will. Yett in time the smarts of your owne rodd will force you to feel it though I weare silent . . . I divers times advised you be more sparinge in your expenses there [in London] that you might spende more liberallie in the countree . . . and spende according to the meanes you had from me till my further augmentation appeared . . . I wish you would learne as your sister Bethell [then a widow] whoe hath not £300 a yeare and yett maintaynes herself and a greate manie children in such sorte as you see.' Since Harry has not taken the trouble to understand the articles drawn up between his father and father-in-law Sir Henry recapitulates them. They comprise an annuity from Lord Fauconberg for his daughter and the greatest part of Sir Henry's estates for any son that is born. But Fauconberg had defaulted and Sir Henry writes that he has 'sent a bill into the Chancerie against his Lordship and their set down the substance of the articles, tho' penned much to my disadvantage whoe hastelie sealed them by candle lyght at midsummer, being necessarilie to goe into Yorkshire the nexte morning.' He suggests that Harry should show the letter to his wife and, if she agrees, that she should assemble the friends of her family and appeal to Judge Hutton to get the matter amicably settled. With what result is not known, but it looks as if Harry's extravagance or negligence or both had caused alarm in both camps.

About this time another of Lord Fauconberg's daughters, Ursula, married Sir Walter Vavasour, the catholic owner of Hazelwood Castle, a pile of white gleaming stone which, from its height, commanded a view eastward from York Minster to Lincoln Cathedral.[9] Here Vavasours had lived since the Conquest and in the chantry chapel, where mass has been celebrated without a break since 1184, are the tombs of two who went on crusade and the skulls of two catholic martyrs, as well as a monument to Sir Walter's father and mother, with all their children kneeling below them.[10] Five years after this wedding the Slingsby-Belasyse-Ingram triangle was completed on a financially sound base when Frances Belasyse married Sir Thomas Ingram, Old Arthur's second son recently 'rescued' from a turbulent love affair in Dublin which Wentworth had terminated by locking him up and sending him home.[11] The newly married couple went to live at Sheriff Hutton.

'Barbara, Lady to Sir Henry Slingsby', in red dress and pearl necklace, (present whereabouts unknown, formerly in the Wombwell family collection at Newburgh Priory)

Sir Henry the Elder, attributed to Vandyck. (*by permission of Captain C. G. E. and Mrs Barclay of Brent Pelham Hall, Hertfordshire*)

Harry may or may not have been negligent over money matters but he seems to have been unfortunate in his dealings with officialdom. He tells how he went to Skipton, 'unto my Lord Chamberlain's house to move his Lordship for the Understuard of the Castle Court of Knaresborough, having formerly his promise; but Robaltome, his man, had changed his mind and when I came he denyed me; at the same time came Mr Matthew Hutton and obtained of his Lordship the Understuardship of Richmond. I have not yet learnt the way how to prevail, nor what more on my part to be seen than a clear intention and a thankful heart.' Similarly when, two years before, he had tried to get the Survey of some of his lands at Harswell from the Feodary at York his 'success was like to that I ever found amongst such people; nothing satisfactory, but always to another man's advantage if they be not pleased; and yet I offered him £5 to let me have it with me, but that will not do. I must send my man to him at Beverley.' But the Feodary for the West Riding, a Mr Goodhand, was even more unsatisfactory over his survey which 'was thought so unreasonable' that the Court of Wards ordered a re-survey, which came out at £311 less. 'It is an easy matter' comments Harry 'for one in authority to extend the power of it to another man's wrong and prejudice, and the more easy by so much as common practice doth authorise it however reason and nature may condemn it as unjust; he regards not what offence he giveth and thinks himself secure if his authority can bear him out; his predecessor made this advantage of it, why may not he follow his example? . . . God keep every man from being an honest man according to the description that is nowadays made of it.'

Goodhand was an even better hand at manipulating wardships, 'where young children without any parents may be bought and sold, not unlike that law for bondmen which gives them liberty to use them as they list so long as they slay not, and yet notwithstanding if they continue a day or two and die, they shall not be punished, for he is their money; and so are wards now a days made money off, whether in the hands of friends or strangers . . . A lord in this county sold his own grandchild that was his ward to pass him over as ward to another; there are not a few examples of this kind.' One, of which Harry was perhaps not aware, was a request by Sir George Goring (who had once had his eye on Harry as a son-in-law) to Sir Robert Cecil to buy for him the wardship of a Sussex neighbour, 'and if he prove well I would be glad to buy him at the full value, of your Honour, for one of my daughters.'[12]

There were by now, of the Redhouse Slingsbys, one son and six daughters married, which marriages are commemorated in the great staircase built and set up by John Gowland in 1637. This village craftsman lived at Poppleton, within easy riding distance of Redhouse, and no doubt there were periodical visits to his workshop to see how the animal crests, which were to adorn the staircase, were shaping under chisel and paintbrush. The staircase is described by Harry as 'above five feet within the sides in wideness, the posts eight inches square; upon every post a crest is set of my especial friends and of my brother-in-laws; and upon that post that bears up the half pace that leads into the Painted Chamber there sits a blackamore cast in led by Andrew Karne, a Dutchman, who also cut in stone the statue of the horse in the garden. The blackamore sits holding in either hand a candlestick to set a candle to give light to the staircase.'

The name of each owner was painted under his crest. The brothers-in-law have already been mentioned. The wild man with club, though only one cloven hoof now remains, would have been as right for that wild man Metcalfe as the golden cock, now in poor plumage, was for the wealthy Ingrams, or the golden stag's head for the Belasyse-Fauconbergs; the Bethells sported a blue spread eagle, the fighting Vavasours a cock gules armed and combed, and Fenwick, that breeder of fabulous horses, a phoenix in flames. The Waterton otter and Stapylton talbot were unhappily interchanged during the move — and look as if they knew it, for the talbot howls and the otter cringes, each on his wrong post. At the foot of the stairs the Slingsby green lion grasps a white leopard's face, and beside it the Pembroke black wyvern toys with a fleur de lys; for Harry, through his grandmother Mary Percy, was descended from Matilda

Herbert, the first Earl of Pembroke's daughter who married the 4th Earl of Northumberland. The contemporary Pembroke was Charles's Lord Chamberlain and often his host at Wilton where he gave him the best hunting in England. The contemporary Northumberland was Charles's Lord High Admiral. But it was an ill-omened shadow which the Percy crest, the blue lion with silver crescent, cast from the head of the stairs, for Mary's uncle, the 6th Earl, had rivalled Henry VIII for the hand of Anne Boleyn till warned off by Wolsey; her father, Sir Thomas Percy, had been executed at Tyburn for his part in the Pilgrimage of Grace; her brother, the 7th Earl, was executed in York for plotting against Elizabeth in 1572; her younger brother, the 8th Earl, implicated in Throgmorton's Plot, had shot himself in the Tower while awaiting trial;[13] and her nephew, the 9th Earl, spent 15 years in the Tower for suspected complicity in Gunpowder Plot. The doom of the house had not yet run its course. Less ominous was the golden dragon of Cumberland, a scholar despite his martial appearance, and the antithesis of the soldierly Sir William Savile whose white owl looks disdainfully down on the black lion's head of the Fairfaxes. Thomas Fairfax, 'Black Tom', had gone up to St. John's College, Cambridge, five years after Harry came down & then at the age of 16 went to fight in the religious wars in the Low Countries under Lord Vere. In this year of the setting up of the staircase he had married his commander's daughter, Anne Vere, and the pair were to become frequent visitors to Redhouse.

All these crests, in their new paint and posted at correct intervals up the staircase, instead of huddled together as they are today, with the curly-headed little blackamore squatting cross-legged at the corner to light with his candles both flights, would have crowned a noble approach to the Great Chamber as well as creating a sort of animal wonderland for the children who pattered up and down the staircase. But this innocent role did not last long. Within the next decade the animals were at each others throats and a sword had divided the friends and brothers.

1   Anthony Upton 'Sir Arthur Ingram' p. 196.

2   Journal of Nicholas Assheton of Downham (Chetham Society XIV) Dr. Whitaker, 'History of Whalley'.

3   Edmund Deane 'Spadacrene Anglica or The English Spaw' (pub. 1626). This Wiliam Slingsby, a brother of Francis, had travelled in Germany in his youth and drunk the waters there. Tasting a spring near his home, Bilton Grange, he found it 'did excell the tart fountaines beyond the seas, as being more quicke and lively and fuller of minerall spirits, effecting his operation more speedily and sooner passing through the body'. An unreliable local historian, E. Hargrove, confused him with his nephew Sir William Slingsby who, until James Rutherford exposed the error in 1921, was credited with the discovery and, as a seventh son, with the miraculous curative powers attributed to seventh sons. A ballad of 34 stanzas composed in his honour in 1862 by William Grainge ends with the lines:

> 'To some the golden mine is given,
> To some the crown and wine;
> But water – peerless water! –
> O Harrogate, is thine!'

4   Diary pp. 290 – 298.

5   In a letter of 1610 from Robert Delaval to the Earl of Northumberland. C. M. Prior 'The Royal Studs of the 16th & 17th Centuries.'

6   HMC X Report, pt. iv. 110.

7   HMC Salisbury, XVII. 495.

8   HMC Various, VIII, 29.

9   This stone came from a small quarry in the demesne and was used to build the minsters of York, Howden, Selby and Beverley as well as the abbeys of St. Mary's, York and Thornton, Lincs. J. J. Cartwright 'Chapters of York History', 367–8.

10   The chapel was spared in Elizabeth's reign because of her love for Ann Vavasour, her maid of honour. The martyrs were a priest, Father Snow, who was hanged, drawn and quartered, and Robert Grimston, a layman who harboured him and was hanged, both of them in York in 1598. Under the altar are the remains of the child martyr, St. Lucy, which Pius IX gave to Sir William Vavasour for his help against Garibaldi in 1867. Hazelwood Castle is now the property of the Carmelites. 'The Tablet'.

11   Anthony Upton, 'Sir Arthur Ingram'.

12   HMC Various VIII, 29.

13   The 8th Earl, before shooting himself, is said to have remarked that 'the b . . . . h (meaning Elizabeth) should never have his estate'. T. Pennant 'Tours to and from Alston Moor' 110.

The 9th Earl, a Protestant who had fought the Armada, was a patron of the arts and a keen mathematician and pursued his studies in the Tower where he was known as 'Henry the Wizard'. He died 11 years after his release on the Fifth of November, still haunted by the Plot! Collins' Peerage.

Chapter Four

1634 – 1638

HARRY, IN WRITING HIS DIARY, modelled himself on Montaigne who, as he says, 'kept a journal Book wherein he day by day registered the memories of the historys of his house, a thing pleasant to read when time began to wear out the rememberance of them. I do likewise take his advise in registering my daily accidents which happens in my house, not that I make my study of it, but rather a recreation at vacant times, without observing any time, method or order in my wryghting, or rather scribbling.' This 'scribbling' covers the years 1638 to 1648 and was first published in an abridged edition by Sir Walter Scott in 1806, and again by the Reverend Daniel Parsons in full in 1836. But, as the original had been lost, Parsons had to use a copy made in 1715 by one of Harry's grandsons, Sir Savile Slingsby. Parsons included a number of family letters and 'A Father's Legacy to his Sons' which occupies 40 pages and was written in prison. Quite recently however the original MS of the Diary has been traced to the Manuscript Department of Nottingham University. It is in excellent condition and freer from spelling mistakes and other inaccuracies, and franker over the diseases the author and his wife suffered from, than Parson's expurgated edition.

The Diary opens with the death of a young nephew of Barbara's, Edward Osborne, son of Sir Edward, Vice-President of the Council of the North and Lieutenant-General of the King's forces in Yorkshire. He was killed on the last day of October 1638 in the gales that had been

blowing most of the month, but 'chiefly upon that day . . .
I hapned to go to York when I had sufficient experience how
boisterous the winds were, being hardly able to sit on
horseback, and as it blew south west it carried the very water
out of the river in a shower over land, and when I came to
York, this unfortunate accident was told me.' The gale had
blown down seven chimney shafts on to the roof of the room
at Kiveton where the boy was having a French lesson. The
tutor escaped, with 'small hurts', and Edward's little brother
was found safe under a table, clutching the kitten in his
arms which he had been trying to catch – a practical
example of how Morrison Shelters, constructed like steel
tables, were to save so many from falling debris in the last
war. This tragedy affected Harry deeply, as one can tell
from the description he gives of this gentle and lovable
boy; and affected even more his wife who, 'having been
warned by this accident would not let me rest till I had
pulled down a chimney that stood on the garden side at
Redhouse which was high built and shaken with the wind.
She would often say how much cause we had to bless God,
that hath given us this warning and not made us examples
to give warning unto others. She is by nature timorous and
compassionate which makes her full of prayer in the behalf
of others. I have sometimes been awaken in the night when
I have heard her praying to herself, as she never mist that
duty in the day time.'

Harry refers again to these gales after describing 'a point
of husbandry, new grown in fashion, of burning the swarth
they mean to plough, the ashes whereof by experience they
find to yeild a greater increase of corn than any other manure
of lime, marl or dung, but it will not last longer than the
taking of three crops, and many think it doth hurth the
ground; but hereafter I will try it upon a peice of ground
which they call the Out Gang[1] being never before ploud in
the memory of any man.' The swarth was cut by a heavily-
weighted sledge-like implement drawn by oxen; this was
then ploughed 'with a broad sock which turns up the sod;
then they gather it into heaps and burn it, then spreading
it upon the land they plough and sow it. The gain is great
they make by this husbandry.' But all this burning up and

34

down the country, he adds, 'may be the cause of so great winds as we have had this whole year that hath done so much harm, both by sea and land'. So scientific experiment was even then blamed for bad weather! Of the thunderstorm this same year that struck Widdecombe church during Sunday mattins he comments 'there is no event that hath not an Almighty providence to direct it, for God is the author of every action and event; but to go about to find out the cause of every accident would be great presumption, being hid amongst the secrets of divine will; who amongst men can know God's counsell and who can think what God can do? The battle is not always to the strong, nor the race to the swift, for time and chance happens as well to the wise as foolish, neither can we judge of the man by such unfortunate accidents as may befall him . . . Some in these days would ground and establish our religion upon the prosperity of our enterprise, as if our beliefs had no other foundation than what is grounded by events, which must needs be a very tottering foundation when every cross accident which comes contrary to our expectation shall hazard the overthrow of our faith. As it hapned to the papists at Black Friars not many years ago in the reign of King James, where they were assembled at mass, the chamber having been overburdened by the multitude of those that came to hear mass, did on a sudden fall down and the fall slew the priest and many others; so this accident at Withicom gives cause of speech to many that were better let alone, and their cause rather maintained with the true foundations of verity.'

By the end of this year, 1638, the Slingsbys had two children, a boy and a girl, and a third was on the way. The eldest, Barbara, had been born in 1633, five years before the Diary started, and the only records of the royal visit that year are a tantalizing remark in the Fairfax Correspondence – 'we have noticed some of the doings at Sir Henry Slingsby's'[2] – and the statue of the horse the Dutchman made and two shield-shaped stones with a saddle and set of horse shoes carved on the one, and on the other an inscription 'He did win the Plate on Achomb Moor in 1633, the King being present.' They mark the grave of this horse on the mound, and bones found beneath them suggest that it was one of those Barbs or Arabs that Sir John Fenwick was then importing to improve the breed. The bed the King slept in, with its blue silk damask hangings with a tufted fringe of silk and gold was preserved at Redhouse till the last century when it went, either into the auction room or to some descendant of the family.

This same year, 1633, had also seen the loss at sea of Harry's uncle, Sir Guilford, Comptroller of the Navy;[3] and in July of the next year Sir Henry received a letter from his other sailor brother, Sir William, who wrote from London : 'I have sent by James Mould, the master of a brigg of Hull, my tombe packt in two great sugar chests. I have paid the frayghte to Hull and the master hath covenanted with me to send upp these goods of mine to Yorke.' He asks Sir Henry to see that it is sent on by water to Borough-bridge and thence 'by wayne' to Knaresborough, 'to be layd in the chapple where my father's tombe lyeth . . .'[4] It survived the sea voyage and journey by barge up the Ouse, past Redhouse, and overland to the family chapel in Knares-borough church. Sir Henry had already had his own tomb set up, noting in the account book 'eighteen pence for ayle and cakes to those that helpte to gett my tomb into the church and for taking down the church wall and making it up again'.[5] Both tombs were by that fine craftsman, Epiphanius Evesham, and represent, though in very different ways, the men they commemorate.[6] For William, who survived his brother by a few years, stands at his ease in hat, buff coat, breeches and boots, a tranquil expression on his bearded face which matches the inscription at the base : 'I go, not tired of life nor yet afraid of death.'[7] Henry, following the then fashionable style of Dr Donne's tomb in St Paul's, is shown pulling the shroud off his lean face as he rises from the grave at the sound of the last trump, blown by an angel, and the summons 'Come ye to Judgment'. The message of the monument eluded the local historian who wrote that this figure, wrapped in wet drapery, must repre-sent Sir Henry's brother Thomas who had been drowned in the Nidd – an observation which would have either amazed, or amused, Sir Henry, one does not know which.[8] We have only his letters, which do not reveal much sense of humour, and two portraits – a miniature by Hilliard when he was 35 and a full-length, reputedly by Vandyck, in his old age – to judge him by. The miniature, now in the Fitzwilliam Museum, Cambridge, shows him three-quarter face, with steely eyes, a pursed-up mouth and the suspicion of a moustache and beard of that colour seen to better advantage in the full foxy beard of his cousin, the 9th Earl of Northumberland – 'Henry the Wizard' – whose miniature lies alongside in the cabinet. In the later portrait he is a formidable figure in black cloak and ruff, broad-browed, grey-haired and bearded, a quizzical look in his searching eyes and what may, or may not be, a smile on his lips. It was painted possibly when he was Vice-President of the Council of the North, appointed by Wentworth, with all that strong man's authority behind him. 'Lett them know', wrote Wentworth when there was some trouble over protocol with the Lord Mayor and City of York, 'that by vertue of my Presidentshipp, doe I preseade all Earles, nay all subjects within the Jurisdiction, and as myselfe, soe the Vice President in my absence.' And so, we may be sure, he did.

But his days were drawing to a close and William's request was among the last of many that had reached him throughout his long life, requests that ranged from appeals for money or promotion in their careers from his nephews[9] and for help in the administration of the Percy estates while the 9th Earl was in the Tower, to the settlement of a £5 debt of a friend's son which was multiplying daily while he lay in the Marshalsea 'where the company may easily make a young man worse addicted.' On 17 December, 1634, the old knight died, aged nearly 75, at the house of his niece and her husband, George Marwood, then living in Nun Monkton Priory. The Priory overlooks the ferry and the wide pool, placid in summer, swirling and foam-flecked in winter, where Nidd joins Ouse. From its upper windows Redhouse can be seen, and the field path that links Redhouse with the ferry, the last view of this world Sir Henry may have had as his life ran out like the river, past his old home.

The household at Redhouse at this time comprised thirty persons 'whereof sixteen are men servants and eight women . . . Our charge is much every yeare at one certaintie, being well accompanied with good and faithfull servants so that at least I spende every yeare £500.' Where some of this money went may be seen in the household account books : nineteen shillings 'for one tonne of Scoch cooles, and 2d to a fellowe to helpe in with the cooles' ; servants' wages ranging from £4 to £1 per annum ; 'necessaries for the kitchings', two rolling pins for the cook at 1/- apiece, ginger bread prints at 1/-, butter prints at 6d, maple trenchers at 10d each ; for one month's washing of shirts, scarves, hose, cap linings and rubbers the laundress received 4/2 ; orders for the garden included winter pears, apples, grapes, apricots, cherries, peaches, quinces and roses. The only entries for food, which normally came from the fish-ponds, deer park or dovecote, are for a fat cow and half a score of fat sheep ; and for the farm, seed-wheat and rye and yokes of oxen.

Slingsby, (as he will hereafter be called) like his father before him, believed in a sound education. When his eldest son Thomas was only four he committed him 'into the charge and tuition of Mr Cheney whom I intende shall be his schoolmaster, and now he doth begin to teach him his primer ; I intend he shall begin to spell and read Latin together with his english, and to learn to speake it more by practise of speaking than by rule' – what is today called the Direct Method. He already knew the Latin words for his clothes and parts of his body, but the next year his father finds him duller – 'but I think the cause to be his too much minding Play, which takes his mind from his book ; therefore they do ill that do foment and cherish that humour in a child and, by inventing new sports, increase his desire to play, which causes a great aversion to his book.' He should have seen some of the 'playway' methods of today ! In all this he says he was copying Montaigne who, at the age of six, could speak more Latin than French. Anyone who cares to read Montaigne's essay 'Of the Institution and Education of Children' will learn that even the workmen and servants in his household became 'so Latinised that the townes round about had their share of it.' This was never so at Redhouse where even plain English was not always comprehended by the indoor and outdoor staff.

We meet some of the staff in the pages of the Diary. There was Francis Oddy, the family upholsterer, honoured by having his head 'carved in wood like a Roman head which I caused to be made for him that keeps the chambers and hath charge of the wardrope, as a rememberance of him that hath so long and faithfully served; a man of very low stature, his head little and his hair cut short, his face lean and full of wrinkles, his complection such that it shows he hath endured all weathers; whose disposition is not suteable with the rest of his fellow servants which doth either by diligence breed envy or else thro' plain dealing stir up variance; and having a working head is in continual debate.' Then there was Thomas Richardson, the steward and keeper of the household accounts, who 'always made his accounts streight to a farthing; if he did misreckon he took the loss to himself;'[10] Ann Richardson, housemaid, who 'so tempered her thrift as to please the servants as well as her Lady and Mistress;' Ann Kirk, her sterner successor, who 'did only apply her thrift in good housewifery to please her Mistress without any respect to the servants which doth make her less beloved by them;' the gardener, Peter Clark, who 'was for no curiosity in Gardening, but exceeding laborious in grafting, setting and sowing, which extream labour shortened his days' (and not 'the great worm in his gutts that did knaw and torment him' which the postmortem proved to have been a delusion); Thomas Adamson, butler and brewer who was to follow his master all through the war and has as memorial the grove of sycamores (or their descendants) which 'he set in the year 1649 by the Green which many yeares ago had been the site of the house which is now called Redhouse.'

The cooks get a page to themselves. 'Last Sunday my Cook George Taylor went to be marryed to a maid of Doctor Wickhams at York, and if she be as headstrong as they say she is he will after find his service here freedom in respect of that bondage he must undergo. This Cook hath been the freest from disorder of five several Cooks which I have had since I became a housekeeper; some of which hath been without all measure disordered. When they have sometimes stolen abroad I should not hear of them for three or four days together; yet commonly I never parted with any of them till I made them as glad to begone as I would have them. I never grew passionate with them, nor threatened them much if I found them serviceable otherwise, but still sought to win them from the habits of drinking by fair means, willing to accept their future promise of amendment, which I took so often for satisfaction, and they every time less able to perform, the habit growing yet more upon them, that rather than they should not enjoy the vice of drunkeness with more quiet and freedom, they would at last be glad that I would take occasion to turn them away. I required not of them so much their dressing the meat, having a woman servant that took into her custody all the provision, & delivered it out, so that I need not fear the Cook's imbezzling especially if he be a marryed man as this Cook Samuell was; and for their curiosity in the art of Cookery I do not much value, nor have we much use for it in our country housekeeping, unless sometimes we have a meeting of friends, and then only to comply with the fashions of the times, to shew myself answerable to what is expected, and not out of any love unto excessive feasting which is now a days very much practised . . . That which blinds every one that they cannot see any deformity in such excess is the generallity of it when it once comes into fashion; whereby we stray from ourselves and seek our evils out of ourselves, when they are rooted in us. I am not sumptuous say we, but the Citty requires great charges; so whilst we perceive ourselves not to do amiss, to recover ourselves will be more difficult.' Sumptuary laws are useless for, by 'prohibitting any man but princes and great persons to eat dainties and wear rich cloaths, they do but increase their credit and price. The best course were to begett in men a contempt of them, as vain and hurtfull things . . . It was a good invention of Seleucus, to reform the corrupt manners of the Locrines, to enact that none should wear any jewels of gold, precious stones or embroidery except she were a profest whore . . . And so should we be easily reformed and made to give over all superfluities if the court did not give reputation to such things, and encrease our longing by their practising.' He wrote feelingly having experienced Charles

I's visit only ten days after the birth of his first child, Barbara. Such royal visits put a great strain on the resources of those country houses selected. Even Sir Arthur Ingram, one of the royal hosts, 'the inventory of whose dishes was as long as the country mile.' had to ask Lord Fairfax to send him 'some herons, of which I hear your Lordship hath great store . . . and send them soon so as to make them somewhat fat against the time.'

An occasional visitor to the house was the ex-puritan Prebend of York, Timothy Thurscross, with whom Slingsby used to discuss religious problems of the day. 'He is a man of late greatly mortified, having within less than this half year resigned unto the Archbishop of York his Archdeaconrie and Vicaridge of Kerby Moorside, being much troubled in his conscience for having obtained them thro' symonie, and now living at York hath nothing to maintain himself and his wife withall but his Prebend. He preacheth every Sunday at one place or other where most need is, and oftentimes on weekdays, and his wife betakes herself to get her living by teaching young children to sew. He is a man of most holy life, only he is conformable to the church discipline that now is used and to those late imposed ceremonies of bowing and adoring towards the altar. When I asked him his opinion concerning this, and that I thought it came too near idolatry to adorn a place with rich cloaths and other furniture and to command to use towards it bodily worship, he answered that his bowing was not to the altar but to God especially in that place, which gesture, he said, was frequently used in primitive times, and every one may do as he is persuaded in mind . . . This man bestows a great part of the day in prayer with much fasting ; he riseth at 4 o'clock in the morning and is at prayer in private and with his family until six, at which time he goes to the Minster prayers and from thence to the Librarie till ten, and then to the Minster prayers again ; and thus he spends his days and strength, being much impaired and weakened by his much fasting. His discourse does much tend to shew how hard a thing it is to be a good cristien, and he that will be a right cristien must suffer martyrdom, if not by loss of life, yet by the loss of credit and honour, which is as dear to many as life itself, seeing we have experience that they will venture life in defence of honour.' It was in the Minster Library that the two men first met and Thurscross there presented Slingsby with a copy of 'The 110 Considerations of John Valdesco,' just translated by his friend Nicholas Ferrar and exquisitely bound by the Ferrar sisters in that other household of practising Christians at Little Gidding. Redhouse was not as anglican as Little Gidding, though Lady Slingsby, 'intending to receive the holy sacrament, and being also great with child, did send for Mr Ascough, a preacher in York (whom she had a very great esteem for) that she might receive from his mouth the absolution of the church and some wholesome council for her soul, he being a man very eloquent both for his ordinary preaching and private discourse. It is a doctrine but of late practised, tho it hath been tought always in our church, the benefit of confession in some cases.' Slingsby however doubted its efficacy 'unless the absolution of the priest did so far opperate as to make the party absolved to stand in no more need of absolution concerning that sin,' because temptation would fall on deaf ears. 'Lime that hath once been slacked, tho' you cast never so much water upon it you can't heat it ; such a change God's spirit may work ; but where such a change is not, there may be a relapse unto the same sin again, and by custome that which at first did overawe the conscience to restrain it, to wit shame, may at last become no restraint at all when custom has made it familiar ; and if absolution should be denied them, and they could not have it at the hands of one they might have it at the hands of another.'

The expected child was born on 14 January, Slingsby's own birthday, and was christened on the 29th in the chapel The godparents of this infant, called Henry, were John Belasyse's wife, Sir Hugh Cholmondeley and Henry Belasyse, but Lord Fauconberg 'would not suffer his son to be a partner with Sir Hugh for some disgust his Lordship had taken at him,' so Henry Bethell deputised. A happier surprise that day was the arrival of Thurscross who had walked the 5 miles from York – a pleasant walk, partly by the river, and better for body and soul than the bumpy drive

up the lane which visiting preachers today have to endure –
after having 'with much ado obtained leave from the
Chancellor Dr Eardell' to preach. He took his text from
'the Gospel for that day where our Saviour commands his
disciples to suffer little children to come unto him and forbid
not.' Though the chapel was not then consecrated 'we
venture to have sermons now and then, altho' we incur some
danger if it were complained of, it being contrary to the
orders of the Church . . . Yet it would be of great ease to us
who live here at Redhouse to have a sermon in the chapple,
being so far from our Parish Church at Moor Mountain,
especially in winter weather.' In this matter of consecration
Slingsby's puritanical leanings are evident. 'It is not amiss
to have a place consecrated for Devotion' he writes 'but we
cannot stay ourself here, but must attribute a sanctity to the
very walls and stones of the Church; and herein we do of
late draw near to the superstition of the Church of Rome,
who do suffer such external devotion to efface and wear out
the inward devotion of the heart . . . Men are prone, if they
be suffered, to turn devotion into superstition, and place it
in the splendor of outward things.' Nevertheless, as has
been already mentioned, he succeeded in getting Bishop
Morton,[11] once his neighbour when vicar of Long Marston,
to consecrate the chapel.

1   This field is still called the Out-go.
2   Fairfax Correspondence I, 281.
3   Sir Guilford married Margaret Walters of York. They lived at Bifrons,
    near Canterbury, and had 8 sons and 4 daughters. Of the sons, Guilford,
    Robert, Walter and Arthur will figure in this story. Margaret is the 'old
    Lady Slingsby' of Pepys' Diary.
4   Letters to Sir Henry the Elder, now in the Folger Library, Washington
    (Folger MS Xd 428) as part of the Cavendish-Talbot MSS.
5   Y.A.J. 1944, 373.
6   Pevsner, Yorkshire – West Riding, 295.
7   Sir William married Elizabeth Board of Board Hill, Sussex. They lived
    at Kippax, near Leeds, and had 2 sons and 1 daughter who married John
    Villiers, elder brother of the Duke of Buckingham. Henry, the second
    son, will figure in this story.

8   Hargrove, 'History of Knaresborough', 1789. In his 1832 edition he
    assigns the monument to Sir Henry, but still says he is wrapped in wet
    drapery. The unwillingness of heirs to carry out their parents' wishes was
    all too common, witness Benedick's remark in *Much Ado about Nothing* —
    'If a man do not erect in this age his own tomb ere he dies he shall live no
    longer in memory than the bell rings and the widow weeps'. Act V, Sc 2.

9   Robert Slingsby, Sir Guilford's son, writing in 1631 to thank his uncle
    for his 'many favours and care for my preferment', continues: 'Yet I do
    not dispayre of imployment ere long because the King is abuilding of
    divers shipps; in the meantime I have partly attained to the Spanish
    toung, that if any Embassador should be sent thither, I might be fitt to
    attend him'. Two years after writing this letter he was made Captain
    of 'the Eight or Tenth Lion's Whelp' to guard the Narrow Seas; and in
    1638 actually did escort the Moroccan ambassador from Portsmouth to
    Lisbon. CSPD 1631–3. 546. Hollond 'Discourse of the Navy'. Folger MS

10 There is a brass to him in Knaresborough church which reads 'Thomas
    Richardson, Gentleman, of Scriven, steward to the Slingsby family, who
    died 28 June 1683 aged 71 . . . full of years and honest fame'.

11 The Bishop was translated from Lichfield to Durham where he preached
    to, and lavishly entertained, the King on that journey to Scotland which
    had been broken at Redhouse in 1633. When Parliament abolished
    episcopacy Morton retired to Easton Maudit, the home of Sir Christopher
    Yelverton, one of Slingsby's friends and Preston's pupils at Queens',
    where he died in 1659, aged 95. He had been 6th in a family of 19.

The lions, by John Gowland, and the leaden Blackamore, by Andrew Karne, on the staircase at Redhouse. Top left, Northumberland lion; top right, Slingsby lion; bottom right, Fairfax lion.
(*Photograph by Ronald G. Sims*)

Letter from Henry Percy, 9th Earl of Northumberland, written 26 July 1613 in the Tower where he had been since Gunpowder Plot, to his 'very loveing friend and cousin' Sir Henry the Elder.

(By permission of the Folger Shakespeare Library, Washington, D.C.)

Letter from Sir William Slingsby, written in London in July 1634 to Sir Henry the Elder at Redhouse, quoted on page 36.

(by permission of the Folger Shakespeare Library, Washington, D.C.)

Chapter Five

1638 – 1639

ONE EVENT of this year 1638 not mentioned by the author of the Diary is the Baronetcy of Novia Scotia conferred on him. These titles were said to have been created about this time in order to give their recipients an interest in Scotland. But the recipients were all too soon to be interested for a reason not intended. For whilst Slingsby and Thurscross were still discussing where Laud's reforms might lead to, Charles came to York on his way to fight the Scots whom his folly has aroused. From the Minster tower, whose 270 steps he had climbed to admire the view, he would have seen that tract of open moorland, whin-covered, part marshy, part sandy, that was to be the scene of one of the most decisive battles in English history, and the beginning of his own downfall – Marston Moor. The Scots had signed the Covenant 'in defence of the government of their church by the Presbytery and to resist that form of publick prayer and administering the sacraments' enjoined by the king. 'They are become most warlike, being exercised in the Swedish and German wars; and from hence many begin to call to mind a prophecy which did foretell that after England had been conquered by the Danes, Saxons, and Normans at last it should be conquered by the Scots.'

Slingsby went, 'out of curiosity, to see the spectacle of our publick death,' to Bramham Moor to watch the training of the light horse to which body he had had to contribute two horsemen, at a cost of 2/6 a man and 2/6 a horse per day. 'These are strange, strange spectacles to this nation in this

45

age, that has lived thus long peacably, without noise of shot or drum and after we have stood newtrals and in peace when all the world besides hath been in arms and wasted with it; it is, I say, a thing most horrible that we should engage ourself in a war with another, and with our own venom gnaw and consume ourself . . . Neither the one nor the other can expect to receive advantage by this war where the remedy will prove worse than the disease.'

War cures nothing and 'if it continue any while we shall not be able to distinguish the sound from the sick . . . We seek by war to defend the Lawe, and while we do so we do but enter into actual rebellion against her own ordinance . . . I desire not employment at these times.' Yet employment came. 'My Lord Deputy of Ireland sent his letters unto my Lord Mayor of York and to myself as Deputy Leiutenants. My Lord Mayor had a commission, but I had no other but his Lordship's letters; by which I sat to assist my Lord Mayor in the taking the view of arms, the which I did perform most diligently, a thing not usual with me who does little effect business; therefore as I entered upon it by virtue of my Lord Deputy's letters directed to my Lord Mayor and myself, after 2 months' service I gave it over, being left out by the Vice-President in a general summons to all the Deputy Lieutenants.' This seems to have disappointed him for he goes on to moralise, not very clearly, on 'abstinence from doing, which is often as generous as doing', and how 'those actions are most commendable that are performed with no ostentation, but on the contrary we judge them lost if they be not set out to show, like mountebanks that show their skill upon scaffolds in view of all passengers that more notice may be taken of them. So ambitious are we of renown that goodness, moderation, equity, constancy and such qualities are little set by.'

To act, or to abstain from action, were soon to become mere debating points, for events were moving fast beyond any man's control. Yorkshiremen, who were all too soon to fight each other, joined the king with the arms for which they were assessed. Slingsby, with two light horse, was attached to Lord Holland who had been made Lord General of the Horse at the Queen's express wish, full of misgivings

46

both about 'this war where the remedy will prove worse than the disease' and about his household whom he had left in the grip of measles, 'a general sickness at this time and few places free from it.' All the children and many servants had it and, though Dr. Vodka[1] had said 'there's no danger of the measells if they come well out', one child died, the infant son of John Belasyse. Slingsby says that he 'bespoke a tomb for it in Moor Mountain church where it was buried, being the father's desire having but this one child.' It had been christened in the chapel the previous December, the god-mother being Anne Fairfax whose husband, Sir Thomas, was soon to be ordered up to the Border with the 160 dragoons — the Yorkshire Redcaps — he had raised.

The only casualty Slingsby mentions occurred as they were riding out to exercise one morning when one of Lord Lovelace's men 'pulling down the cock of his pistol, gave fire to the wheele and shot the man before him cleare through the head peice into the head, so that he fell back dead upon his horse.' Nevertheless his first experience of soldiering Slingsby found 'a commendable way of breeding for a young Gentleman . . . for as idleness is the nurse of all evil, infeebling the parts both of mind and body, this employment of a soulgier's is contrary unto it; for, by enabling his body to labour, his mind to watchfulness, and so by a contempt of all things but that employment he is in, he shall not much care how hard he lyeth, nor how meanly he fareth. It will learn him to be dutiful and obedient to his commander without reply; and it makes one not over fond of this life, but willing to resign it.' Slingsby himself lay neither hard nor fared meanly, having a room allowed him in the house of his cousin, Sir William Selby, at Twizel, which Holland had made his headquarters 'and there kept a very noble house and gave great entertainment to many of the Commanders that frequented to him . . . Thus were we quartered, the Horse at Twizel and the Foot in the camp at Hockley, and the King's pavilion and the Noblemen's tents upon that part of the camp which is called Yearford-more . . . All this while the Scots not a witt daunted at this preparation, nor came there any of them to make submission but rather made their preparation to resist according as we came nearer to them.' No one had much idea what sort of preparation this was 'untill they were seen from our camp to encamp themselves at Duns, which the King with a perspective glass discovered' – and had some pretty rude things to say about the Intelligence. And doubtless about Holland who, when ordered, with 1,300 horse and 2,500 foot, to seize and hold some defence works which the Scots had thrown up at Kelso, left his foot floundering over the Tweed 3 miles behind and rode on with the horse to the top of the hill above the enemy position, alerted the garrison who marched out to meet him, 8,000 strong, protected by intervening 'marrish ground and hedges' and covered by their 'peices of ordinance so planted that we could not come near them' and then, like the Duke of York, gave orders to march back again down the hill to the jeers of the Scots, 'without medling at all with them.'

The day after this fiasco Slingsby received an urgent message from his wife who sent the butler, Thomas Adamson, to say 'she was desirous to see me, for she was in a great fitt of sickness.' He took post and reached Redhouse in 24 hours, only to find her well again. 'It was a wind which tormented her, being gott about her stomach and midriffe did so dilate it that it put her in intolerable paine.' Before returning to the Border he settled a three-year-old dispute with the Vicar of Knaresborough, a Mr Rhodes, who had taken his presentation to the living from the Prebend of York, Mr Smelt, instead of from Slingsby who was the patron and had promised it to another. Rhodes's predecessor, Broadbelt, had died while Rhodes was on his way to Chester for institution by the Bishop, and this had complicated the issue. For, as Slingsby claims, 'I declared that Mr. Rhodes came in upon resignation and not upon the death of the incumbent; he pleads that he came in upon the death, for all that we had a copy of the presentation and institution all which mentioned it to be upon resignation.' As Rhodes had held the living on either count for three years however, he agreed, 'to put an end to all differences', and pay Slingsby his legal expenses (which amounted to £110) 'and thereupon took his presentation from me.'

The day after Slingsby's return to Twizel, June 18th, another but less satisfactory agreement was reached at Berwick-on-Tweed between the King and Nobility of Scotland — 'if that can be called an Agreement' as Clarendon comments, 'in which nobody meant what others believed he did.' The army dispersed and Slingsby started for home once more and on the way met Thomas Hinks, his gardener, 'post with the like message from my wife, of her relaps again into her old disease; so I left mine own horses and took post, and at my coming home her fit was past, and she pritty well recovered; and so hath continued till now, the 10th September, that she hath begun again and in some more extremity than the former. It did at first puzell the physitians to understand what she ailed. They thought it had been the Cholick, then the Jaundize, then the Spleen; and every one gave her according as they judged the disease. Dr Parker gave her a vomit, but after this she had fainting fits in her stomach; and, her pain increasing, I sent for Dr Micklethwayte and he judged it to be the Jaundize and thereupon administered a drink which instantly eased her pain, which was so violent that for two days she was scarce able to sit up, continually having one to hold her side . . . She had before this last fitt symptoms which confirm that her malady is from the Spleen; whereupon hearing of Dr Fryars, a physitian of London, of his being in the country, I sent unto him at York, my brother Sir Arthur Ingram being about to come to my house with my sister and my wife's sister. They brought the Doctor with them whose chief art it is (as he saith) to cure the Spleen.' His prescription was steel pills for four or five mornings, taken after a dish of broth with cream of tartar in it, and then for a week morning and evening, 'with exercise, ascending to nine or twelve spoonfuls of Rubar pouder, and after that heat wine and drink it after some beare.' He also prescribed 'pills of castor each other night to be taken bedward against fumes,' and 'Holland pouder whereof to take the weight of a groat or sixpence in posset ale some mornings instead of the Rubar pouder.' The beer was to be taken 'hot at meales, first boyled, then scummed, putting to it a sprig of sea-wormwood to strengthen the stomach.' Though this doctor boasted of his £50 and £100 cures and his royal and noble patients, he inspired no confidence in his latest patient who, as her husband says, 'expected no other than death, and so did she express herself to me & to others. As she lay awaken in the night she would spend the whole time in discoursing of her latter end, making a recollection of all her sins and working upon herself a hearty sorrow for them. And finding the apprehension of death terrible, she would say she desired nothing so much as that God would give her a willingness to die whensoever he should call for her; and that she might attain to it she would make use of all the promises which confirm her faith and cause her to see a vanity in all earthly things.'

He breaks off to describe the construction of a wooden gable to the chapel to replace the heavy brick one which was on the point of bringing down the whole end of the building, in spite of a buttress his father had caused to be built and the 'underhiving' of the sides with long timbers and binding the gable end to the roof with iron bolts by 'an ingenious workman, but a drunkard and one that went in his apparel more like a bed'am than a workman.' Having seen the wooden gable finished he and his wife, by then somewhat recovered, and Barbara 'went to see the rotten house at Scriving and to order for the repair of it.' Scriven, near Knaresborough, had been the home of his grand-father, Francis, and here they spent two nights 'having neither bed nor furniture but what we borrowed of my tenants, Ch. Maye hanging blankets for curtains, and so making as good shift as we could. We lay in that Chamber which is called my Lord of Northumberland's, he that was beheaded for raising a rebellion in the North in the reign of Queen Elizabeth, being the first that lay in it after the building of it, coming to see my grandmother, his sister. ' Extensive plans for repairs and alterations were discussed with a freemason, to include a new staircase at one end which would serve both the old house and the new wing he intended to build – for he believed that 'not only should we please ourselves in that which we build, but do it at a time when we may best enjoy it . . . and not like him who, when he is a-going to his grave, puts marble out to work, to build brave houses.'

'But', he continues, 'I am taken off my intention of building for a while with the preparations I make for a journey to London; my wife, not perceiving any recovery of her health after so many tryalls with physitians of our country, desires to go to London where the best are, not only for the cure of the spleen, but to advise concerning the scrophula or swelling which lay so near her throat that she feared it might grow to choake her, and it encreased her fears being told of a young woman that lately died, being choaked with the big swellings on each side her throat. We took our journey the 2nd of December leaving all those provisions we had made for our accustomed keeping of Christmas; and in twelve days we got to London, but we rested at Mr Capell's house in Hertfordshire for a day, and had tarryed longer for to refresh my children, my son Thomas and my daughter Barbara, which we carryed with us, but an unexpected accident hindred us, coming thither when the gentlewoman of the house big with child, expected every hour to be delivered. I presumed of a welcome from the master of the house, for that intimate acquaintance and league of friendship that was between us when we were fellow pupils at Cambridge.' They went on to stay at Great St Helens in Bishopgate, where a new Doctor, Geford, came with Dr Fryars to see Lady Slingsby. 'They gave her physic, but no great amends she found by their rules. The physitian commonly favours himself more than the patient, and is more sure to find that which shall do him good from the patient he undertakes than can the patient be sure to find any good from him; therefore it concerns him to extoll his skill above any experience he hath. He professes to cure all manner of diseases and his practise is but his tryall, he never attains it. If his practise were upon himself I should the rather venture, but he would not pay for his skill at so dear a rate, tho' he foold us to venture on him.' Plato, he continues, is said to have thought that a doctor should have had all the diseases he attempts to cure in others, for 'they make such descriptions of our infirmities as doth a town cryer who cryeth a lost horse, or a dog, and describeth his stature, his hair and ears, with other marks and tokens; but bring him to either and they know him not. They promise much but perform little, and less than all other arts do they shew the effects of what they do profess.' After dropping Dr Fryars they were advised by Sir Lionel Talmash, himself a surgeon, to try a lady doctor, 'Mrs Kelway, wife to one of this Lord Keeper's secretaries; she practised chimistry and out of that art had extracted certain oyles and saltes which she applyed to all diseases; and having made it her study for 20 years together, and with much labour and cost attaining to this medicine, she persuaded herself it must do all things; she would give it inward for any disease, or apply it to the side for the spleen, sewing up a certain quantity thereof in a taffity bagg, so applying it upon the spleen. But after a month's tryall my wife, finding no good at all, she gave her over, bestowing on her for her pains a diamond ring. Old Sir Arthur had had the like tryall of her medicine for the spleen but no better success.' Two more doctors, Baskerfield and Ruthen, were consulted, and finally Sir Theodore Mayerne, the king's physician, 'and from him she hath reaped the most benefit for her health. The course he took was after purging she was to take a julep made with Lignum Neophriticum for 6 dayes together; then to purge again and after that to apply a fomentation to her belly for other six mornings; then to bath and drink asses milk and now and then to take a purging electuary'.

---

[1] "A Polish doctor, described in list of former recusants' subscriptions as 'MD practitioner in physics St Saviour's York'" Subscription Book R.IVe. B2. A letter is extant from Sir Henry the Elder to Vodka's father, also a Dr. Alexius Vodka, who died and was buried in St. Saviours, York, in 1626. Add MS 29681 f.276.

Chapter Six

1640 – 1641

WHILE THEY WERE IN LONDON Slingsby had been elected one of the M.P.'s for Knaresborough 'thro' the diligence of my man Thomas Richardson, to whom I committed the whole carriage of it, and went not down myself to be at the election, which gave my competitors, Sir Richard Hutton and H. Benson, the more advantage against me; but my man's care prevented their subtile plots. He hath served me ever since my father dyed, being a man of great integrity and of indefatigable pains and industry who formerly had served my father.' Slingsby sat in that parliament which opened on 23 April 1640 and was dissolved three weeks later 'without having done anything to content either King or country.' The King wanted money for his Scottish wars and parliament debated whether to demand redress of their grievances or 'supply the King first and take his word for the latter.' Their main grievance was the imposition of Ship Money 'which the House had voted to be absolutely against the law if the King had not sudenly dissolved the house of Parliament.' Certain M.P.'s had their trunks and pockets searched and three, who included Henry Belasyse and Sir John Hotham, 'were committed to the Fleet for their undutifull speeches to the King at Councill Board.'

Before setting out for Yorkshire at the end of June the Slingsbys were entertained by Lord Holland at his house 'at Kinsington, at which church I had been marryed to my wife about 9 years agoe.' Slingsby was 'much taken with the curiosity of the house [the building of which had been largely financed by Sir Arthur Ingram] and from it I took a conceite of making a thorough house in part of Redhouse which now I build, and that by placing the dores so one against another and making at each end a balcony that one may see cleare thro' the house.' He and his host would have also had much to say, as well as to leave unsaid, about their military service on the Border. The family got back to Redhouse on 3 July, 'returning with all those we went out with excepting one boy whom I left to be a prentise, a son of Widow Barker's of Scriven ; and in his stead I hired a Cook which I brought down with me. At my coming home I found my building here, and at Scriven in good forwardness, the first floor being laid.'

In a less healthy state were political affairs. The king's army, once again marching against the Scots, was billeted around York and the king had asked that it might be maintained there for fourteen days. 'On the 28 of July,' writes Slingsby, 'being the assize week, I went to York where the Gentlemen of the County intended to meet to consult together of an answer to return to the King . . . Hereupon they petitioned and pleaded their inability, and hoped the King would lay no such burdens upon them considering they so willingly and chearfully had served him the last year, in which service and other militant expences they had expended £100,000.' When the King reached York on 23 August, he summoned the Gentlemen, assured them that the money would be paid back, and asked how soon the trainbands could be raised, 'for he intended to lead them and be their General.' The Gentlemen replied that 'they could not get them to stir' unless they had 14 days pay in advance. This the king refused, expecting that the county would pay the men for two months. The Gentlemen said they would consider this if the king would call parliament.

At this point of deadlock, and on hearing that the Scots had captured Newcastle, Slingsby, who had already seen enough of their military efficiency, decided to take his wife and family and his sister-in-law, Lady Vavasour, to the safety of John Belasyse's Lincolnshire home at Worlaby – 'a bizarre brick house, with decorative details of the weirdest.'[1] But the crossing of the Humber from Hull to Barton was more terrifying to the little party than the menace of the Scottish army. High winds, rough water and a collision in the harbour mouth which nearly sank them caused the ladies 'to cease not weeping and praying till we came ashore at Barton' and Thomas 'to cry vehemently as if he would have burst himself, and pray as heartily. His mother had taught him to say his prayers, but I dare say he never prayed to God before.' Lady Ingram, Slingsby's sister, met them with her coach and drove them on to Worlaby, but he himself returned to Hull, and on to Beverley 'to see the old Minster and Monuments [the Percy Shrine and tombs of his ancestors] and so dined at Weighton; it is strange to see how the wayes are pestered with carriages of all manner of preparations for warr; 30 peices of ordinance I met coming from Hull, and abundance of wagons, with all things belonging to pouder, shot and match, tents, pikes, spades and shovels. It was too late to march with their train of Artillery, for before they could get to New-castle the Scots had possessed themselves of it. And now the whole country of Northumberland and Bishoprick of Durham are compelled to pay contribution money to Lesly, the Scots General: £300 a day they demanded of the county of Northumberland, and £350 of the Bishoprick of Durham.' For victualling the army they demanded '30 thousands weight of bread a day, 10 tuns of bear a day, 6000 weight of cheese, £50 worth of beef and £34 worth of mutton a day. We come not yet in Yorkshire into contribution with the Scots, for they have not yet invaded us; but notwith-standing we feel the burden of the warr as well as our neighbours, by those regiments of foot and horse that are quartered amongst us and about us, and the trainbands. The King's army consists of 19,000 foot and horse, and the trainbands of the county 12,000 which the county hath maintained above a month.' When some of Slingsby's tenants were asked to pay their assessment – four nobles a man – they asked if they had to pay their rents as well. 'But all this charge hath been to no great purpose, for they did lye idle being billeted about York, and when they had been at all this charge, they were sent home again.' What with impositions and taxes and the wastage of the country-side by the soldiers 'men are at a stand what course to take, or how to dispose of themselves. The fear they apprehend by that which hath befallen their neighbours in Durham and Northumberland [where Sir John Fenwick had "£15,000 worth of horse flesh gone by the Schotts Army in one morning"][2] hath made many here to forsake their houses, so that it is greatly to be feared we shall find both the value of our lands and rents to fall very much.' So far, Slingsby says, he has 'escaped very well, having no manner of loss,' and his plough lands 'lett dear about Knaresborough' yielded up to 18/- an acre. At this point in the Diary some-one has for some reason neatly cut off the rest of the page. So we leap from one of Slingsby's ploughed fields on to the slippery floor of the Great Hall in the Dean's house in York where, on 24 September, the king and his Council of Peers were met 'to consult what answer to give the Scottish petition, and how the King might have a supply of monys to maintain his armys in the meantime.' Sixteen peers were appointed as commissioners to meet, at Ripon, such com-missioners as the Scots should appoint, and John Belasyse was detailed to carry the proposals to Newcastle. As for the money, the City of London was asked for a loan of £200,000 – and responded with £30,000. Within a week the Scottish lords had reached Ripon where Slingsby went 'out of a desire to understand how things would go.' The parley broke up after three weeks, the English agreeing to the Scots' demands for £25,000 a month for two months 'to maintain their army about Newcastle till all things were agreed on in our English Parliament.' Lord Holland, a better host than soldier, 'kept his Table at Rippon for all the Lords, and the Scots commissioners sometimes were invited by him.' Thurscross had been appointed 'to wait on our English Lords, who bestowed his pains in preaching to them, but some of them disliked the minster service and refused to come, in better agreement to the Scots.'

On 13 October Slingsby went to Knaresborough for the parliamentary elections and found himself opposed once more by Sir Richard Hutton and Henry Benson. 'When it came to poleling I carryed it, but with some difficulty, and

Henry Benson.[3] Sir Richard Hutton laboured all he could to carry it by the industry of his father's man Moore who dwells in the town, and I likewise by the diligence of my man Thomas Richardson who took great pains to bring the burgesses together which he knew would give their votes for me, he himself being one. There is an ill custom at these elections to bestow wine in all the town, which cost me £16 at the least and many a man a broken pate.' On 2 October he left for London, riding up in company with other M.P.'s, and got there in five days. 'Great expectation there is' he notes 'of a happy Parliament where the subject may have a total redress of all his grievances.' All delinquents, projectors and 'monopolizers, such as levied Ship Money and such Judges as gave it for law' were to be questioned; and 'all innovators either in church or state, and as cheif actors therein they fell upon my Lord of Canterbury and Strafford and accused them of high treason.' Parliament was in a strong position, backed by the Scots army occupying Newcastle till money was found to satisfy them, and this money would not be found unless bills for 'preventing the untimely dissolving of Parliament, and another for tryennial parliaments and for the taking away the High Commission and Starr Chamber Courts' were passed. Peace with the Scots 'proved a business of great difficulty not easily effected, like the tossing three balls in one hand which requires both the eye and hand to be very steady.' A poll tax to raise the necessary money was at last agreed on, Slingsby's share amounting to £30. Some wished to lay hands on the lands of the bishops on the pretence that they had made new canons contrary to law, and this gave Slingsby an opportunity to declare his views on the episcopacy in general. He was in favour of the bishops losing their vote in the house of peers but opposed to removing them altogether which was the 'business cheifly aimed at by Parliament and solicited by our countrymen that live beyond the seas in Holland, hoping that if episcopacy were abolished they might peacably live at home and enjoy their consciences.' He did not think that the government of the church by bishops was 'of such absolute necessity that the taking away of them should quite overturn the state and essence of the Christien church;' but he did think that their removal would endanger the peace of the church. Even the apostles had not believed in 'parity amongst all presbiters,' some, such as Timothy and Titus, being above the rest in dignity. Moreover the common people would 'think themselves loose and absolved from all government when they should see that which they so much venerated so easily subverted.' Many of those who were opposed to the episcopacy pretended it was because of its misgovernment, but might it not be because they disliked others being 'preferred before them?' If all ministers were made equal 'in a few years there would be as great contention between those that are learned and unlearned as now there is betwixt those that are preferred to honour and those that are not.'

Slingsby spent 14 weeks in London staying in rooms at 12/- a week, and regularly went to see Sir Theodore Mayerne about his wife's health, sending down to Redhouse the medicines he prescribed; 'for his custom is to register in a book the diseases of all his patients, if there be difficulties, so that sending for his book he finds what he hath done to her formerly, and thereupon prescribes the same. Usually I went in a morning for his advise, about 7 of the clock, where I used to find him set in his study, which was a large room furnished with books and pictures; and as one of the cheifest he had the picture of the head of Hyppocrates, the great physitian; and upon his table he had the proportion of a man in wax, to set forth the order and composure of every part; before his table he had a frame with shelves whereon he set some books; and behind this he sat to receive those that came for his advise, for he seldom went to any, for he was corpulent and unweildy;[4] and again he was rich, and the King's Physitian, and a Knight, which made him more costly to deal with all.' Nevertheless his treatment proved effective, for Slingsby makes no further mention of his wife's health when he got home, only that she had 'married Anne Richardson to Mr Fish and taken Ann Kirk to be her housemaid in her roome.'

On 30 March of the next year, 1641, he went up to parliament again, taking his wife as far as Temple Newsam 'to see his sister Ingram who the day after our coming fell sick in labour and delivered of a son. This I carryed as news to her husband who was then at London.' In this session of parliament the Bill of Attainder against Strafford was passed. Slingsby was one of the 59 out of 263 M.P.'s who opposed it and had their names posted in Old Palace Yard as 'Straffordians', enemies of the commonwealth who should also perish. The Fairfax Correspondence notes that 'after 14 weeks' attendance in the stormy atmosphere of Parliament Sir Henry Slingsby returned to the super-intendence of his buildings and other domestic avocations,' and did not again take his seat and so was voted unfit to attend and was succeeded by Mr Stockdale. Nevertheless he had remembered, in the midst of that stormy atmosphere, to send from his London tailor an Easter present of a suit of breeches and doublet for five-year-old Thomas whose mother 'had a desire to see him in them, how proper a man he would be.' It might have been a presentiment on her part for towards the end of the year her illness returned and another journey to London was planned. But first they went to say good-bye to her parents at Newburgh where one more doctor, recommended by Sir John Fenwick's daughter, was summoned from Newcastle; 'but after a weeke's tryall he returned, having given him six peices for his pains of coming, but little good in point of cure.' Just before they were to leave for London their coach was 'robbed and all the lining, fringe and lace taken out, upon All Saints Day at night; but we, being so near our journey, must be glad to go up with it as it was, only making use of some curtains which was pinned up for a poor shift. The 11th of November I set forwards towards London with my wife and children' – a date that was to be as fixed in his memory as it is in the memories of many today. To the modern traveller in a 'luxury' coach the four or five-hour run from York to London is quite an ordeal. The decision to take a wife as ill as Barbara was, and two young children, on a twelve-day journey in a comfortless coach (there were no glass windows) over rough roads in mid-winter must have been a desperate one.

It was to be their last journey together, for on New Years Eve, 'after she had endured a world of misery, her many infirmities turning to a consumption,' she died at Monsieur Sebastian's house in Covent Garden. A post-mortem revealed 'decay in every parte and her lungs in the upper part extreamly imposthumated. The loss of her by death is beyond expression, both to her children and all that knew her ; but cheifly to my self who hath enjoyed happy days in her company and society which I now find a want of : she was a woman of a very sweet disposition, pleasant and affable, and a very tender and careful mother of her children ; and when anything moved her to anger, or that she conceived any injury done to her, she would easily forgive, and be the first that would offer termes of reconsilement ; and tho' she was passionate, it was not lasting but soon passed over ; she was exceeding timerous and fearfull, which made her apprehend many dangers to herself; she would say she was not affraid to dye, but of the paines of death ; and to her physitian she would say she desired nothing to prolong her life so she could have any thing to ease her pains. So it happened to her as she feared, for certainly she dyed a very painful death, having the use of her speech and senses and memory to the very moment she dyed. Now what loss is to be compared to my loss ? The Lord hath sent it to me for not valuing so great a blessing in a wife ; and I will now comfort myself in this hope that the Lord hath taken her unto himself, and . . . given her an inheritance with his saints in light, where is light and no darkness, joy and no sorrow, peace and no war, felicity and happiness without misery ; to which place I hope in God I shall once be brought. She would always be calling to have some part of the Scriptures read unto her, and cheifly the Psalms, and the night before she dyed she said by heart some part of the 103 Psalm. Her cheif worldly desire was that my daughter Barbara might have a portion set forth, which I did, in case I marryed, by a deed which I sealed to, and gave my brother John Belasyse to keep. I buryed her upon the altar steps, unto the south side next my Lady Savils in the Parish of St Martins Church, which had been our first meeting and our last parting ; I marryed at London in anno 1631 the 7th day of July, and lived the first year in St Martin's Lane, and so kept my first Christmas in St Martin's Parish ;[5] so is our lives and

Tomb of Sir Henry the Elder in the Slingsby Chapel, Knaresborough Church. In the foreground are the effigies of his father and mother. (*By permission of the Parochial Church Council.*)

Photograph by Ronald G. Sims.

Tomb of Sir William Slingsby, by Epiphanius Evesham, in the Slingsby Chapel, Knaresborough Church. *(by permission of the Parochial Church Council)*
Photograph by Ronald G. Sims

purposes disposed of by God Almighty.'

He came down from London in May with John Belasyse and his wife who took eight-year-old Barbara on to Newburgh while he went to his widowed sister, Mary Bethell, with Thomas and his tutor, Mr Cheney. Henry, then only three, is not mentioned. 'I had not been yet at my own house,' Slingsby writes, 'not abiding to come where I should find a miss of my dear wife, and where every room will call her to my memory and renew my grief. I therefore stayed at Alne untill I had better digested my grief.' Alne Hall, now a bright and airy Cheshire Home, stands on rising grounds above the tiny river Kyle where Thomas would soon be trying to catch fish. One wonders whether Anne had succeeded in getting a good preacher to occupy the new pulpit in the church. Of sermons in stone there were plenty for young and old in the fabulous creatures from the Bestiary carved round the arch of the Norman porch.

1 Pevsner, Lincolnshire. 431.
2 HMC X. Pt iv, 110.
3 Henry Benson was expelled from parliament next year for selling 'protections' to persons not his menial servants. He was imprisoned in York Castle where he died in 1643. Y.A.J. 1939.
4 It was only a desperate message from the King, campaigning in Worcestershire in June 1644 – 'Mayerne, pour l'amour de moi allez trouver ma femme' – that drew him from London to find the Queen in Exeter, where he delivered her daughter, the Princess Henrietta, "Minette". Next month she escaped to France and never saw the King again. C. V. Wedgwood, "The King's War".

5 Old St Martins church was pulled down in 1721 and rebuilt in the classical style by James Gibbs. The vaults in the crypt were piled high with coffins, some of which were claimed by relations and removed. The remainder were reburied in the St. Martin's Cemetery, Pratt Street, Camden Town, among them presumably Lady Slingsby's since there is no record to the contrary. Sir Theodore Mayerne, the only doctor who had brought her any relief, died in 1655 and was buried in the church, as also were his wife and five children. There is a monument to him in the crypt of the present church. J. McMaster, 'St. Martin's in the Fields'. 102.

Chapter Seven

1642 – 1644

THE LIVING of Knaresborough had fallen vacant again, and the Prebend of York, Dr Eleazar Duncon, hearing rumours of Slingsby's choice of a successor to Rhodes, went to see him at Redhouse, whence he was directed to Alne, but missed him again. So on 16 June he wrote with some urgency to say that he was right glad to hear Slingsby had asked their mutual friend, Thurscross, 'to nominate a fitt man for that place' and hoped he would 'persist in that way and not present on the suddaine; for you need make noe haste for feare of mee presenting one before you, as I heare my predecessor did' – the scheming Smelt – 'for I believe you have the full and only title, to which I submitt with my former humble request to you for an able and a sufficient man in all respects. The towne stands in neede of such a one in regard to the largeness of it, and the great resort to it in summer time by reason of the wells.' The living was worth £100 a year, and 'many a Bachelour in Divinity in either University will readily accept of it, who will discharge the place to your good liking and mine. And you know, Sir, it highly concerns us two (who have the Glebe and great Tithes there) to provide to the best of our power for the good and commendable discharge of that cure.' Though he says he has 'noe designe upon any particular man' he clearly had a strong objection to the man Slingsby was reported to be considering – Mr Cheney, Thomas's tutor. 'I beseech you, Sir, even for God's love to his Church not to give it to him,

62

unless you in your owne conscience be perswaded upon good grounds that he is able in all points to discharge the place to the honour of God and the edification of his Church.'[1] Whether Slingsby was, or was not, so persuaded his own future had been unexpectedly changed when he received a commission to command the trainbands of the City of York. This meant leaving young Cheney behind in a puritanical household in remote Alne, with only one small boy to look after. He may have seen the Knaresborough presentation as a happy solution, both for Cheney and the parishioners of Knaresborough who, in the past few years, had had one ailing vicar and another who lasted only five years. By the time he received Duncon's letter however he was in York in the midst of his new and exacting duties, for the train-bands were trained in name only. Cheney was not appointed but the man who was, Roger Atye, was there only three years and had to resign at the end of the war.

At about the same time as Slingsby reported for duty in York a certain Captain Hodgson[2] began his Memoirs, which were destined to be bound up with that edition of the Diary abridged by Sir Walter Scott. 'When I put my hand to the Lord's work,' wrote the Roundhead Captain, 'I did it not rashly, but had many an hour, day and night, to seek God to know my way.' The Cavalier Colonel does not tell us in so many words how he found his way, but Clarendon says 'he was swayed only by his conscience to detest the violent and undutiful behaviour of that parliament . . . and when he could stay no longer with a good conscience in their counsels, in which he never concurred, he went into his country and joined with the first who took up arms for the King.'[3]

His first duty was to take twenty of his very amateur soldiers 'to be a guard to the King's person during the time of his abode in York; but I perceived a great backwardness in them, and upon summons few or none appeared, so this was passed over and no more done, for the King went to Beverley to be near Sir John Hotham and his son, who refused him entrance [to Hull 2 months before] with that train he came withall.' The Gentry and inhabitants of Holderness, 'your most loyal and oppressed subjects', had petitioned the king to relieve them of the burdens imposed by Hotham and especially 'this last attempt of cutting our Banks, drowning part and endangering the rest of the Levell of Holderness which is a Presumption higher than was ever yet attempted by any subject to our knowledge.'[4] The king's reply to this petition, delivered to him at Beverley, was to promise aid both by Proclamations and force. 'Therefore he gathers together part of the trainbands,' Slingsby continues, 'and with my Lord Linsey cheifly in command they make some show to block up the town of Hull, and cast up some works, burn down the mills, guard the river, make cannon burketts and blinds; but without effecting much he returns to York.' This was a serious blow to Charles for Hull was the largest magazine in the country as well as being the most convenient port for receiving supplies from the Queen in Holland – as she herself repeatedly pointed out in her letters. Charles had already lost the navy, and with it command of the seas, partly due to the lethargy of Northumberland, his Lord High Admiral, all but six of his Captains (of whom Robert Slingsby was one) having gone over to Parliament, for which action Robert and another Captain were imprisoned.

The king now considered marching to Nottingham, but first he summoned the Gentlemen of the County and the freeholders to meet him on Heworth Moor, but at different times. The Gentlemen he advised to hold the county 'for he believed after he was once gone out of Yorkshire they should find Hotham would pour out an army upon them (for that was his very word).' The freeholders' meeting 'produced nothing else but a confused murmur and noise, as at an election for Knights of the Parliament, some crying the King, some the Parliament.' Charles then left Yorkshire, having given out many commissions, 'but none in rediness; my Lord Crawford had spoken to the King for me to have a commission for a regiment of foot, but the King had so many that waited for employment that unless I would find arms for them when they were raised, it would not be granted.' The supreme commander now was the Earl of Cumberland, Lieutenant of the North, whose capacity for such a post had been gauged by Strafford three years before when he wrote

64

'You must practise the pike, my Lord, so much a day. I wish I were at your elbow . . . Exercise your men. Rouse up that old Clifford virtue that is in you !'[5]

As Charles had prophesied Hotham marched out of Hull and, with scarcely any opposition, into the West Riding where he made the Leeds men pay him what was intended for the royalist Governor of York, Sir Thomas Glemham. This young Hotham 'was a very vigilant soulgier, made long marches, and often in the night he would march 16 miles to take a delinquent out of his bed.'

While the Gentlemen raised money and levied men by commission of array, Sir Thomas Fairfax continued to live in his house in York, but one evening he sent his man after Slingsby, as he was riding home to Redhouse, and warned him that what he and the Gentlemen were doing was 'against law & caused the county to be in fear.' Slingsby replied that 'neither he nor any of his had any cause of fear, seeing as then he had not appeared in arms, and that what was intended was against Hotham, who ranged the country and would not keep in Hull.' A few days before this encounter General Ruthven, the septuagenarian commander of Scottish troops in the Swedish army, and twenty two of his Scottish officers returning from the German wars, spent a night at Redhouse on their way to Skipton. It was said that when Gustavus Adolphus wanted to regale his political opponents and extract secrets from them 'in their more cheerful hours, he made Ruthven field-marshal of the bottle and glasses as he could drink immeasurably and preserve his understanding to the last.'[6] One hopes the Redhouse cellar was equal to the occasion. Slingsby went with him as far as Knaresborough where some of his tenants told him that Lord Fairfax was about to occupy the castle. Ruthven advised him to anticipate this move, 'whereupon I got the keys of the Castle, caused a bed to be carryed in, and that very night comes Sir Richard Hutton and part of the trainbands with commission from my Lord Cumberland ; so I returned and only lay in the Castle that night, and in the room and lodging that was built by my father and where I had lain when I was very young, being sent for by my father' – possibly at the time of Gunpowder Plot. Slingsby had formed a high opinion of the Scots as soldiers and obtained the General's consent for two of his officers to be attached to his regiment, 'unto whom I sent £30 intending to make one of them my Lutenant Collonell of the train-bands of the Citty and Ainsty.' But Cumberland would not allow it and also insisted on his hereditary right to transfer to himself, as Captain of Clifford's Tower, 200 men, which so-called honour 'made the regiment little worth.'

Fairfax now came out into the open and joined Hotham, and together they 'blockt up York,' Fairfax from the west, Hotham from the east, 'whom by the time it was light day you could see facing the town with a Troop of horse and sending a jeer that when he comes he finds them still in their beds.' Fairfax was as active, 'beating in our scouts and taking some prisoners, and my man, his horse and arms was one of them that was taken prisoner.' One officer even rode up to Micklegate Bar, shot a townsman in the neck and rode off again. In another part of the town a colonel, leading his dragoons in on foot, was shot at and missed by a captain, on horseback, whom the colonel pulled off his horse by his sword-belt. They were fighting it out on the ground when their troops joined in; the colonel was butt-ended into the ditch and the captain had his thigh broken 'whereof he dyed – a sore scuffle between two that had been neighbours and intimate friends.' The Gentlemen at last sent an appeal to 'the Lord of Newcastle to send his army, which he was raising in Northumberland, for our relieve in Yorkshire.' This he did and was welcomed 5 miles north of York by a ceremonial parade 'in batalio of horse and foot and cannon,' on which Cumberland 'delivered up the keys unto him, but not willingly.' He might have been less willing still had he known that Newcastle's soldiers had had no pay since they left Northumberland. 'They hoped to find mony plenty here; but this was the mischief of it. Here was neither treasure nor treasurer; the soldiers must be the collectors.' Newcastle therefore assembled the Gentlemen of York and asked them 'to subscribe their names what every one will lend, and himself begins and subscribes two hundred pounds, and so the rest followed untill it came to my turn to subscribe one hundred.'

Newcastle established himself in Pomfret, thus dividing the parliamentary forces in Yorkshire, and from here wrote to Colonel Guilford Slingsby (the late Sir Guilford's son, who had been Strafford's Secretary) encouraging him to continue levying men for his regiment – and to use his discretion 'as regards the Lady, as the Earl has not been used to taking ladies prisoner,' (though he was soon to find himself in a similar situation). Only a week after this was written Guilford was severely wounded, in a skirmish at Guisborough with Sir Hugh Cholmondeley,[7] and captured; but efforts to save his life by amputating both legs above the knee failed. On him were found Newcastle's orders to collect all private arms and move all gentry and their families and movables into York which was to be made a magazine to counterbalance Hull, and its defences strengthened so that it would be a safe place of retreat for the Queen.[8]

As commander of the Northern Army Newcastle proceeded to grant commissions. Some of those who received them were papists,[9] and one of these was Thomas Waterton who had inherited Walton Hall on the death of his father the year before, and now joined the new regiment of foot Slingsby, his uncle, had on 13 December been commissioned to raise. 'I caused my drum to be beaten up in York and other places,' Slingsby writes, 'and those that came to be listed I caused to be billeted amongst my tenants.'[10] After raising 200 and coping with all the administrative difficulties (complicated by the men's transferring themselves at will from one captain to another) the regiment was ready enough for service to join Newcastle's army on its march to Bridlington where the Queen had just landed with money from the sale of the crown jewels, which she had been loath to part with, 'they looked so beautiful' as she told the king in a letter. This was the end of February 1643, just a year since she had sailed for Holland. Newcastle found her at dinner in a little house by the quay where she spent the night, only to be awakened next morning 'by the cannon thundering from the parliament's ships who, tho' they knew the Queen to be there, yet endangered her very much and ceased not to shoot untill Vantrumpt, the States of Holland admiral who conveyed the Queen hither, sent a message to the parliament ships to wist them give over shooting, for he would be no longer made a looker on.' In the meantime the Queen and her ladies, 'to save themselves from shott, gott under the bank of a little gullet of water that ran into the sea at the harbour, which running deep between two banks gave security to those that sat there; here, having cloakes cast under them and about them did the ladys sit and take notice without danger where every bullet grazed; and yet for all that, a little farther there did lye the body of a soulgier torn and mangled with their great shott.' The bombardment lasted two hours, its main targets the quay and the house where the Queen was supposed to be (and whither she returned in the midst of the firing for a favourite lapdog left asleep in her bed). 'To secure the harbour where the Queen had putt in three ships loaded with arms and ammunition (for they shott amain at them thinking to have fired them) Leivetenant General King had cast up two works on either side of the harbour, and raised two batteries on either side, and two drakes to discharge upon the ships and to hinder their approaching nearer; which when they saw they could do no good upon them, at the next tide they weighed anchor and away.'

The Queen stayed in Bridlington for three days and Montrose and other Scots came to kiss her hand. Another visitor was young Hotham who came, ostensibly to treat with Newcastle about the exchange of prisoners; 'but I believe it was then that he was tryed and offers made him, upon condition, if he would render up Hull to my Lord of Newcastle.' To further this Sir Marmaduke Langdale, an ardent East Riding royalist,[11] was asked to use his influence as an old friend with young Hotham's father, Sir John, who was 'covetous and ambitious, which two vices led him much on to be made Governor of Hull . . . But it was my Lord of Newcastle knew how to work upon his distemper when he once found his pulse.' Slingsby thought it was young Hotham's 'jeering and disagreeing' with Lord Fairfax that made Sir John waver in his allegiance. 'For he was one that was not easily led to believe as another doth, or hold an opinion for the author's sake; for what he held was clearly his own judgment, which made him but one half the

Parliaments; for he was manly for the defence of the liberty of the subject and priviledge of Parliament, but was not at all for their new opinions in church government.' Soon after this the Hothams were arrested on suspicion and sent to the Tower. Their correspondence with Newcastle, captured with his papers after Marston Moor, sealed their fate.

Meanwhile Langdale had been raising a regiment of foot and arming them from the ships, and was now ready to march with the Queen and the rest of the army to York, where she was to stay in Sir Arthur Ingram's palatial house. Slingsby's regiment was left to garrison Stamford Bridge whose Governor, Colonel Throgmorton, had 'made sure of Sir Richard Darley's estate, sowed his land with his own corn, laid a tax upon the country, 3d upon every horseload of corn that passed by his garrison; and thus he kept the town with great vigilance until his excellency commanded him away.' Slingsby succeeded him on 6 May and found himself faced with dissatisfaction among the soldiers who were short of pay and food, and the countrymen who 'came so slowly in with their assessments that the horse belonging to the garrison was employed wholly in fetching it and such persons as refused; and sometimes, making no difference, would injure those that were well affected and duly paid, so that much of it was lost.' During the eight weeks Slingsby stayed there he 'eased the country of that tax which the former Governor had imposed' and substituted a fixed weekly rate to be paid to the garrison, 'for I thought that good usage would make the countrymen pay more easily, having little else to procure him money.'

The Queen was anxious to join the king and a council of war was held at Pomfret to decide whether Newcastle with his army should accompany her 'and give a gallant addition to the King's, leaving the country in Lord Fairfax's power,' or whether he should send only some of his forces and then 'lay siege to Lord Fairfax in Leeds, or fight him in the field. Well, this latter was resolved on.' Newcastle started off by taking Howley House, with Sir John Savile in it (Sir William's parliamentary cousin), and then defeated Lord Fairfax on Atherton Moor, capturing Bradford and driving

Sir Thomas out who joined his father in Leeds, 'ill-accoutred, having broke his stirrop and lost his pistoles,' and found him resolved to fly to Hull and deaf to all argument. For, 'like an old Gamester, he knew the hazard of venturing on still upon hard luck.' So Sir Thomas returned to Bradford to extricate some of the troops left there and, with his wife and five-year-old daughter, 'Little Moll,' made a dash for it. Lady Fairfax was captured, but the child escaped, carried off in a dead faint on the pommel of her nurse's saddle. Fairfax fought his way out of Selby with a bullet through his wrist so that he had to hold sword and reins in one hand, and ultimately reached Hull by a wide detour into Lincolnshire after 40 hours in the saddle; his wife arrived there by coach, with Newcastle's compliments; and the nurse and her charge rejoined them by boat down the Humber.

'We left His Excellency,' continues Slingsby, 'sollacing himself with his victory, which gave new strength, courage and health to every soulgier . . . Now the country was clear to the very gates of Hull, saving only Wressel Castle.' Newcastle therefore made a recruiting march into Derbyshire and then into Lincolnshire, whence he was recalled by the Gentlemen of Yorkshire to deal with the Fairfaxes whose 'shattered troops began to drop in one after another, and what he wanted on foot he made the country supply him with out of the east riding.' It was argued that Newcastle's 'only way would be to besiege Hull; and of that opinion was Lievetenant General King, and it might be won if the Gentlemen would undertake to raise an addition of fource out of the country.' This they did, but 'it fell out to be an ill season to lay siege to that town that lyeth so low and in water, the summer being spent and the season falling out to be exceeding wett.' The king had once asked Sir Thomas Glemham if it could not be starved out by cutting off the fresh water supply but was told that 'the very haven is fresh at low water, and every man can dig water at his door, and they cannot bury a corpse there but the grave drowns him ere it burys him.'[12] Newcastle capped Warwick's comment, that the men in the trenches were likelier to rot than the inhabitants of Hull to starve, with what was considered his brightest remark, 'You often hear us called the Popish army but you see we trust not in our good works.'[13] Nevertheless he flooded the country round Hull by opening the sluices, closed in on the town which he tried to fire 'with red hot bullets, but they did no hurt at all,' and bombard with 'flat bombs which wounded cheifly the earth.' There were sallies 'to beat us from our works and we, attempting to take from them their own works, did no less, but was beaten out of them again.' At last, 'having tyred out his soulgiers with hard duty, many falling sick with cold and wett lying, and few of the arrayed men abiding it, he was forced to give over the siege, leaving behind him one of the great guns that had broken her carryage ; and for want of carryage was forced to burn his boats which he had to march along with him out of Northumberland for the passing of his army at any river.'

The siege was raised on 12 October. This was the second blow Hull had dealt the royalists who thereby lost both the initiative here, and an ideal headquarters in a predominantly royalist east riding from which to campaign against the west riding with its wealthy wool trade. Hull had proved to be all but impregnable except to that side which had command of the sea. Slingsby records a remark made many years before the war by Sir John Hotham, that 'if he had Hull a garison he would be able to bring all Yorkshire into contribution' — words that stuck in his memory, with fateful results.

1 Diary pp. 329–331.
2 'Memoirs of Captain John Hodgson of Coalley-Hall, near Halifax; touching his conduct in the Civil Wars, and his troubles after the Restoration.' The last date in these Memoirs is in September 1683. Hodgson served in Maj-General Lambert's Horse and in Colonel Sanders's Horse.
3 Clarendon, XV 100.
4 Y.A.J. 1902, 240.
5 Wentworth Woodhouse Archives, quoted by Birkenhead in his 'Strafford' p. 216.
6 Harte, 'Life of Gustavus Adolphus', i, 177.
7 Cholmondeley, that godfather of whom Lord Fauconberg had so strongly disapproved, at first fought for Parliament believing that a treaty with the King would be more surely won by the sword than by voting in the House of Commons. Soon after the Guisborough engagement he changed sides and handed Scarborough Castle over to the Queen when she landed at Bridlington. He held it till forced to surrender after Marston Moor.

8 HMC, V Report, 69.

9 Y.A.J. 1930–31, 410. The 'Kingdom's Weekly Intelligence' of 19 January 1643 says that 'Papists in Yorkshire daily flock to his Lordship in great numbers'. William Vavasour was also commissioned at this time and served as a major under his brother, Sir Walter, in his regiment of horse.

10 Fairfax Correspondence II, 263. 'Sir Henry Slingsby raised 600 men, horse and foot, at his own expense and led them in the chief actions of the Civil War'.

11 Despite his royalism Langdale had, as High Sheriff of Yorkshire, refused in 1639 to extort Ship Money, and calmly filed the official warning that unless he raised the £12,000 demanded he would incur 'the utmost of such forfeitures & punishments as by the laws of this realm may be inflicted upon you for so high a contempt & misdemeanour', endorsing it 'Received this letter of Mr Barker 29 May at 4 o'clock afternoon', and put it away. F. H. Sunderland, 50.

12 Surtees Society, Yorkshire Diaries, Vol 65. 134.

13 Warwick's 'Memoirs', 265. Reckitt, 95.

Chapter Eight

1644

JANUARY OF THE NEXT YEAR, 1644, brought more trouble from the Scots who crossed the Tweed and advanced through snow storms on Newcastle to seize it before help could arrive. But 'His Excellency makes all preparations he can to meet them . . . and gives orders immediately for his army to march . . . and his regiment gets into the town the night before the Scots came.' Their first attack was beaten off by Sir Charles Slingsby, a cousin, 'who gave them such a repulse that they forebore after to make any more attempts, but lay at a defensive guard,' despite all Newcastle's efforts to draw them into the open. The Gentlemen in York 'were daily in expectation of hearing some good news out of the north, and hoped that His Excellency before this would have beat the Scots out of Northumberland; they judged it to be like a fray at a Markett Cross, soon begun and soon ended. But long experience hath taught their General wisely to detract fighting, knowing that a victory could not gain him so much as a bad disaster might prejudice.' They had some reason for their impatience for they had to provide for Newcastle's army. To make matters worse 'Sir William Constable crept out of Hull with their Horse, making their carracols upon the wolds' and, in a night attack on the regiments of Sir Walter Vavasour, Sir John Keys and Thomas Slingsby (Harry's brother), took many prisoners. But what put a sudden end to the Gentlemen's moans, 'as a fitt of an ague is cured by a fear,' was the startling news contained in an intercepted letter from Sir Thomas Fairfax to his father

73

in Hull that he was coming from the south 'with recruits and supplys to try his fortune once again in Yorkshire.' John Belasyse, commanding the Yorkshire forces in Newcastle's absence, immediately marched to Selby to prevent the junction of the Fairfax forces, 'but was not able, my Lord Fairfax having the benefitt of the river to pass when and where he would.' Resolving to hold them at Selby, Belasyse replied to their summons to surrender that 'he would not deliver it up to a rebell, which answer incensed my Lord Fairfax and they prepared to storm.' They captured Selby and took a number of prisoners, among them Belasyse who was wounded. He was sent first to Hull and then to the Tower where he remained for 10 months until exchanged.

This bad news brought Newcastle hurrying south, fearful lest York should also fall. 'His coming was diversely received; we in York were glad that we had the assistance of his army, the foot to be put into the Citty for the defence of it and the horse to march to the prince to enable him the better to releive us. The countryman was glad he came with the Scots at his back, for now they said they should pay no more sesments, which was but the hope to ease a galled horse's back by shifting saddles.'

The Scottish and Fairfax forces met on Bramham Moor on 20 April and the two armies, numbering about 16,000 foot and 4,000 horse, proceeded to invest York on two sides, till 'my Lord of Manchester came with his Norfolk men and closed us up on every side. Provisions we had in good store in the town, but mony we had none; which bred us some trouble to help out, and many complaints both from the soulgiers and townsmen. My Lord took a course to have them billeted and proportionately laid upon both the Gentlemen and officers either to find them meat or mony, after a groat a man per diem; which for my share came to £4. 5s. a week, the mony being raised out of the corn which I brought into the town. This fell heavily upon some, that being sojourners and in great want yet was fourced to maintain a soulgier, tho' they were put to the shift to borrow; and their was no remedy, for the soulgier knew him that was appointed to pay him, and if he refused the soulgier lays hands on him or any thing he had.'

Day by day the besiegers closed in and with their cannons 'played continually into the town.' They overran the suburbs and began to mine. Manchester 'works his mines under St. Mary's tower and raises a battery against the mannor wall that lyes to the orchard, and begins to play with his cannons and throws down peices of the wall; we fall to work and make it up with earth and sods.' The mine under St. Mary's tower was sprung on Trinity Sunday by the Scots General Crawford, unbeknown to the other two generals, 'which falling outwards made the access more easy; then some at the breach, some with ladders, getts up and enters, near 500.' But Crawford's 'great vanity alone to assault the breach' cost him 300 men. It also angered Fairfax for the records of all the dissolved religious houses north of Trent, which he had been paying Dodsworth to transcribe, went up with the tower. One wonders if some of those fanatical enemies of popery realised what they were treading on.

Newcastle, determined to resist to the end, had rejected all terms — 'a gentleman of grandeur, generosity, loyalty and steddy and forward courage', as Sir Philip Warwick wrote of him, 'but his edge had too much of the razor in it, for he had a tincture of a Romantic Spirit, and had the misfortune to have somewhat of the Poet in him.'[1] Perhaps it was this tincture which inspired the defence; for they were soon reduced to one meal a day and broadcast SOS fire signals from the Minster towers which were seen at Redhouse and answered from Pomfret. None of the messengers sent to Rupert urging him to hurry to relieve York got through, not even Slingsby's, 'they kept so strict guards as I could not get any in either in the night or day, to go to Redhouse and bring me back word how my children did, but were taken either going or coming.' No news may be good news, but of little comfort to a man in such circumstances.

'But at last he whom we so long looked for was heard of coming to our relief . . . not so believed till we perceived the Scots had drawn off their guards, which our centinells gave us notice of.' All but three regiments — Slingsby's City Regiment and those of John Belasyse and Sir Thomas

Glemham – now marched out to meet Rupert at the end of that brilliant surprise march, as he crossed the Ouse by the bridge of boats built by the Scots, and followed hard on their heels as they withdrew from York. Although Slingsby's regiment remained in York, tradition has it that he himself took part in the battle of Marston Moor, under Newcastle.[2]

The tale of this, the biggest and possibly the most decisive battle fought on English soil, begun in a terrific thunder storm and ended by the light of a harvest moon, has been told and retold and several unsolved problems still face the military historian. This is hardly surprising since within half an hour of the start six generals – three from each side – were in full flight, the battle had wheeled so that both armies faced in opposite directions to those they had started in, and at the end each side thought it had won. One problem however, that of the exact position of the Scottish foot in the battle, has at last been solved, thanks to the chance discovery[3] in 1967 of a much damaged letter written on 5 July 1644 in the Scottish leaguer – 'a just copie', the writer says, of another he had sent to Lord Loudon, the Lord Chancellor. This letter to Loudon, which was printed anonymously as a broadside in Edinburgh under the title 'The Glorious and Miraculous Battel at York', and reprinted 200 years later by James Burns in his 'Scotland-Historical Fragments', was the letter Sir Charles Firth quoted from in his account of the battle.[4]. Had he seen the original he would have learned that the writer was Sergeant-Major-General Sir James Lumsden, commanding the Scottish foot, and also that he himself had correctly placed the Scots on Fairfax's right and not on his left as some other eminent historians, following Captain Stewart's 'Full Relation of the late Victory', had done. For Lumsden appended to his letter a plan of the parliamentary order of battle, with a key, the first contemporary parliamentary plan to have come to light. And even though he apologises for 'the brigads drawn up heir . . . not so formall as it ought to be', it is formal enough for an accurate reconstruction to be made,[5] something Firth was not able to do.

Lumsden gives his Lordship an account of the victory God had bestowed on them after they had abandoned the

foote disposed of w.th most aduantage to fought some of them
Drawne of, to line the hedge of the corne feild, where the
enimy must come to charg. The enimys forces consisting
of 3 parts the Scotts Manchester and Fairfax, weare one
mixed w.th an other. Crumwell hauing the left wing drawne
into foure bodys of horse, came off the warrant by Bilton
breame to charg our horse, and vpon the first charg routed
them, they flie along by wilstrop wood side as fast and as
thicke as could bee, et our left winge prest as hard vpon there
right wing, and pursued them ouer the hill. After our horse
was gone they fall vpon our foote, and although a great while
they mountained the feight yet at last they weare cutt downe
and most part ether taken or kild. Here J lost a nephew
Coll: John Fenwicke, and a kinsman S.r Charles Slingesby
both of them slaine in the feild, the former could not be
found to haue his body brought of, the latter was found and
baried in yorke minster. The enimy pursued not but
kept the feild as many as was left, for they weare fled as
fast as we, and there 3 generalls gone thinking all had bene
lost. we came late to yorke w.ch made a great confusion: for
at the Bar none was suffered to come in but such as weare
of the Towne, so that the whole street was thronged vp to
the Bar w.th wounded and lame souldiers, w.ch made a pitifull
crie among them. The Prince the next morning marches
out w.th the remaining horse and as many of his foote men
as he could horse leauing the rest in yorke w.ch weare
entertained into seuerall regiments as well to haue
them to doe duty, as to prouide for them quarter and Billett.
Prince marches out at Muncke bar and so north ward to
ward Richmond, where he w.th Coll: Clauering w.th some
forces comming towards him: my Lord of Newcastle
and Leift Generall King to: Scarborow where they too ke
shiping to goe beyond sea. thus weare we lost at yorke
out

Letter, dated 5 July 1644, from Sgt.
Major-General Sir James Lumsden
to Lord Loudon describing the
battle of Marston Moor and
appending a plan of the
parliamentary battle order (see
Appendix 179–81 for transcription)

siege of York on the interception of that order from the King to Rupert 'that nothing but Impossibilities should stay him from beating the Scots' – an order Sir John Culpeper prophesied would be the King's undoing. They found Rupert, writes Lumsden, 'drawing up in ane plain feild 3 myles in length and in breidth, the fairest ground for such use that I had seen in England.' But they could do little for the next two hours, till the foot came up, except hold the ridge with the horse and advance the cannons 'to play on them . . . which maid them a littell to move'. Then came 'the advance down the hill throch ane great feild of corne to ane ditch which they had in possession, which it pleased God so to prosper that they were put from it, so that the service went on verie hot on all sydes, we lossing on the right wing and gaining on the left'. Of the Scottish foot in the centre Lumsden names those regiments and their commanders which stood and fought and those which fled 'most baselie . . . possessed with ane pannik fear'. The only Scottish casualties he mentions were Lord Dudhope,[6] Lt-Colonel Brison, two captains and some soldiers. Cromwell and Leslie on the left wing were, he concludes, 'under God ane main occasioun of our victorie'.

Slingsby's account of the battle reads: 'The Prince follows on' (after the Scots) 'and makes an hault at Marston town, the Scots then marching up the field the direct way to Tadcaster; but upon the top of the hill they face and front towards the Prince who, till now, was perswaded that they meant not to give him battle, but to march quite away. Now the Prince bestirs himself, putting his men in such order as he intended to fight, and sending away to my Lord of Newcastle to march with all speed. The enemy makes some shot at him as they were drawing up into battalio, and the first shot kills a son of Sir Gilbert Haughton that was a Captain in the Prince's army; but this was only a shewing their teeth, for after four shots made they give over and in Marston corn feilds falls to singing psalms. The Prince's horse had the right wing, my Lord Goring the left, the foot disposed of with most advantage to fight, some of them drawn off to line the hedges of the corn feilds where the enemy must come to charge. The enemy's forces, consisting of three parts, the Scots, Manchester and Fairfax, were mixed one with another, Cromwell having the left wing drawn into five bodies of horse came off the Cony Warren by Bilton to charge our horse, and upon their first charge routed them; they fly along by Wilstrop woodside as fast and thick as could be; yet our left wing prest as hard upon their right wing and pursued them over the hill. After our horse was gone they fall upon our foot and altho' a great while they maintained the fight yet at last they were cut down and most part either taken or killed. Here I lost a nephew, Coll. John Fenwick, and a kinsman, Sir Charles Slingsby,[7] both of them slain in the feild; the former could not be found to have his body brought off, the latter was found and buried in York Minster. They pursued not, but kept the feild as many as were left, for they were fled as fast as we, and their three generals gone, thinking all had been lost.[8] We came late to York, which made a great confusion for at the barr none was suffered to come in but such as were of the town so that the whole street was thronged up to the barr with wounded and lame people, which made a pitiful cry among them'.

The royalist, Sir Philip Monckton, relates how his horse was shot under him as he led his regiment, 'but soe neare the enemyes that I could not be mounted again but charged on foot and beate Sir Hugh Bethell's Regiment of Horse, who was wounded and dismounted, and my servant brought me his horse'.[9] In the driving smoke he lost his regiment and Bethell (a cousin of the Alne Bethells) probably did the same. 'The runaways on both sides', wrote another eye-witness, 'were so many, so breathless, so speechless and so full of fears that I would not have taken them for men'.[10] There was 'a little foot officer without hat, band, sword, or indeed anything but feet and so much tongue as would serve to enquire the way to the next garrison'.[11] Lord Fairfax is said to have fled home and gone to bed. Had it not been for his son, Sir Thomas, who unhorsed, his face slashed from mouth to ear and without his white parliamentary badge made his way right through the royalist army to find Cromwell, also wounded, on the other flank and there plan to attack the royalist left wing in the rear, there might have been no victory for either side. This historic ride was commemorated by a leather cup made from one of the boots Fairfax had worn.

Over 4000 dead remained on the field, stripped to their 'white smooth skins which gives us occasion to think they were gentlemen' as Parson Ashe wrote. Sir Charles Lucas, who had had his horse shot under him as he charged, and been captured, was taken next morning to select any of the slain for private burial. He wept at the sight that met his eyes, but singled out only one and asked that the bracelet of hair which the dead man was wearing might be returned to a lady who would receive it thankfully. One young wife came from Knaresborough to search for the body of her husband, Charles Towneley, a Lancashire papist, till a parliamentary officer persuaded her to desist and, bareheaded, escorted her off the field and mounted her behind one of his troopers. The officer was Cromwell. Many of the dead would have been wearing new shoes looted that morning from the Scottish army store-barge abandoned in the river at York. The villagers buried them in long graves, briar-covered mounds today, at Four Lanes Meet, Wilstrop Wood, The World's End Nursery and White Syke Close where Newcastle's Whitecoats (who were said to have brought their winding sheets about them) were slain to a man. That villager who, warned off the moor the evening before because of an imminent battle between the King and Cromwell, asked 'Whaat, be they two fallen oot then?' had his answer in full measure. Relics are still ploughed up in the fields and foresters used to find musket balls embedded in the tree trunks of Wilstrop Wood. Today, when a fox is found there, the drumming of hooves and the twang of the horn echo that other grim chase when Rupert's horse 'fled fast and thick as could be' by the woodside, where moss-green horse bones still crop up among the nettly mounds.

Newcastle, with a number more who included Lord Fauconberg, escaped to the coast and took boat from Scarborough. He settled in Antwerp where he started a riding school and wrote a classic – 'La Methode et Invention Nouvelle de dresser les Chevaux' (published in 1657) – thus endorsing the opinion that he was a better horseman than musician, a better musician than poet, and a better poet than general.[12] 'Thus were we left in York', writes Slingsby, 'out of all hope of releif, the town much distracted and every one ready to abandon her; and to encourage them that were left and to get them to stay, they were fain to give out false reports that the Prince had fallen upon the enemy and suddenly routed them, and that he was coming back again to the town; yet many left us, not liking to abide another siege which after began, for the enemy, taking a few days' respite to bury their dead, to provide for the wounded, and to gather up such scattered troops of foot and horse as had left the feild (for by this time their Generals had returned) they were now in readiness to march back again to York'. They mounted new batteries and made a bridge 'to clap over the Fosse and store of hurdles for a storme, having nothing but the ditch, which was almost dry, to hinder their entrance. Therefore thinking it not fitt to hazard the town, having noe hopes to be releived, we capitulate in article and upon that day fortnight the battle was fought, we yeild the town; and that upon very good conditions, if they had been kept. For we were to march out with our army, and with flying colours; to have convoy till we came within 12 miles of the Prince; those that would might tarry in the town; those that would not might have carts provided to convey such household good stuff as they had in the town; to have protection and enjoy their estates'. A number of officers left the army after this. Sir Walter Vavasour was one who went abroad; and Colonel Thomas Slingsby retired to his home and compounded.[13] Not so his brother, wholly committed to the royal cause and perhaps not yet able to face Redhouse without Barbara.

'Upon these articles', he continues, 'we march out, but find a failing in the performance at the very first, for the soulgier was pillaged, our wagons plundered, mine the first day and others the next. Thus disconsolate we march, forced to leave our country unless we would apostate, not daring to see mine own house, nor take a farewell of my children tho' we lay that first night at Hessay, within two miles of my house'. On the second day of their march they reached Knaresborough where they were 'much molested by

Manchester's horse that cast stones at us, and tho' we had a guard of seven troops, yet could they not, or would they not, prevent them from plundering; but in the feild before Allerton Mauleverer where we made an hault till our rear was brought up, we were forced to endure affronts by some of the enemyes that came among us and would snatch the soulgiers' hats from their heads and their swords from their sides, and tho' we complain of it to the officer yet could we have no remedy; and going a little further into a straight lane they overturned the first wagon, which was my Lady Wooton's, and fell a plundering it. Whaley, Cromwell's Leivet: Col: meets us and goes along with us, discoursing of the fight on Marston Moor, desirous to see Sir Richard Hutton, at whose house he quartered, and would fain have invited him to his own house where his Lady was; but he would not; and likewise would have perswaded me to abide at home, shewing how much he desired to shake hands with me. Upon Knaresborough forrest we made a handsome shew with those troops of our guard, for we marched with their colours, but not with above six or seven score men'. Among the colours were nine of Sir Thomas Glemham's and one of Slingsby's, probably bearing the lion rampant.

At Otley the guards left them and they marched on up the dale to Kirkby Lonsdale where they met Langdale and the Northern Horse. Slingsby here left Glemham, who wanted to join the garrison of Carlisle, and went into Lancashire where Sir John Mayney, who was to become his closest comrade-in-arms, had 'a Brigade of horse of broken and shattered regiments . . . Here we found our quarters sweet, not sullied by others trading, having no soulgiers to trouble them before we came'.

1 Warwick's Memoirs, 235.
2 Y.A.J. 1915, 374.
3 An unforeseen change of plan led to two strangers meeting as fellow-guests in a Yorkshire country house, first stranger the author, second stranger Mr H. L. Verry, c.b.e., who had bought the Marston Moor

dispatch some years before, from a London antiquarian bookseller, but had never properly studied it.

4   Transactions of the Royal Historical Society, New Series, XII, 50.

5   But which Brigadier Peter Young is now engaged on doing.

6   Lord Dudhope later died of his wounds. It was said that when Charles was told of his death he remarked 'that he hardly remembered he had such a Lord in Scotland', to which some bold spirit retorted that 'the Lord had wholly forgotten that he had such a King in England'. Anglorum Speculum or The Worthies of England in Church and State, by G. S.

7   Sir Charles had held Newcastle against the Scots in 1643. During restoration in York Minster in the early 1900's his bones and smashed skull were disinterred – and photographed.

8   'General Leslie with his Scottish army ran more than a Yorkshire mile, and a wee-bet'. Anglorum Speculum.

9   Monckton Papers, 17.

10   T. Carte, Original Letters, 55–58.

11   Vicars, God's Ark.

12   Fairfax Correspondence I, 243.

13   He compounded for £350, Y.A.J. XXIII, 374.

Chapter Nine

1644 – 1645

SIR JOHN MAYNEY had quartered himself at Dalton, 4 miles north of Barrow, and the enemy, reinforced with sailors from the ships that lay off Fouldrey Castle, at the top of the Barrow peninsula and approachable only at low tide, determined to drive him out. They attacked with horse and foot but Sir John put their horse to flight and drove the foot 'to the very sides of the ships,' taking 200 prisoners whom he sent to Rupert but keeping 'seventeen sailors and some rich country men, whom the prince had given for exchange, in Dalton Castle to make their advantage by randsome or otherwise.' He followed this success up with a night attack on Northscales, on Walney Island, which could be undertaken only on an ebb tide, and then in less than six hours. But his horse were observed drawn up on the sands and a volley made them run, killing the horse he was riding which was the horse Guilford Slingsby had been killed on at Guisborough. He attacked the next day but found the enemy gone and so burnt Northscales to the ground, sparing only a stone house whose owner had been a royalist and 'when he dyed had charged his sons upon his blessing not to take up arms against the King.' Mayney now 'had all the country men at his devotion. When he summoned them they appeared and would bring their monys upon his warrant, being part of the King's rent.' A thousand were ready to serve the king and Slingsby was surprised that 'they could do so much, namely to furnish 1000 men and pay £2000, notwithstanding the many losses they received pay £2000, notwithstanding the many losses they received by troopers.' Mayney paid the horse with this money and sent £1,000 to Glemham at Carlisle, to be kept for the Prince's use. The next time he called them together was 'to list them under severall Captains and have them keep their guard at Ulverston.' This they agreed to do but were unwilling to serve outside their own county. At this assembly an old parson, once a Roman Catholic, preached to them, 'his pulpit a huge stone which he leaned upon, the country men standing round about him very attentive,' and his theme was 'to dehort them from Rebellion.' For this he was given £50 which represented his pension from the king and was paid by Mayney from the rents he had collected.

Soon after this the parliament ships were ordered to leave Fouldrey and go to support Sir John Meldrum in the siege of Liverpool. 'So we removed our quarters from Dalton to Mr. Preston's house at Holker,[1] where we had extream good entertainment; a house free for all comers and no grudging at any cost, tho' we eat him up at his table, and the troopers in the feild stealing his sheepe and not sparing his corn that stood in the feild. And here we took our pastime and would go out to hunt and course the dear.' At one time they contemplated fortifying Fouldrey Castle 'and went to view it but we found it so ruinous, nothing remaining but the walls and part of them washed away with the sea; and tho' it might be made a harbour for shipping, yet the channel lying too far distant the Castle could not command it.'

It was then decided to march out of Lancashire with the forces that had come with them and others that had since joined them. They hoped for a troop of Captain Jackson's (Cumberland's Quartermaster in York) but 'he played fast and loose with us' and, pretending that a high tide prevented his baggage from making the 12 mile crossing of the sands from the Lancaster side of the estuary, went to join the enemy. There is still enough local legend of disaster on this crossing, where the tide comes up with a bore, to make travellers, even when travelling light, think twice before attempting it. Even among Mayney's officers there was no unanimity. Some wished to march to Rupert at Chester, but were persuaded to stay if they could join the Gentlemen of Westmorland whom Mayney went to meet at Kendal, but received little encouragement. So he offered his services to Glemham, but Carlisle was so close beset by the Scots that Glemham had had to send his own horse away to Skipton – and was starved out of Carlisle the next year, having eaten all the horses that remained[2] and earned the name of being 'the first man that taught soldiers to eat cats and dogs.'[3]

No other course was now open to Mayney except to follow Glemham's horse. They accordingly set out on 10 September 'and by marching in the night passed thro' the enemy that lay on every side.' A skirmish near Ingleton lost them one Lieutenant of Horse; and a false alarm at Settle 'caused out horse to draw back above a mile, but when it came to be understood, it was but a row of trees which they took for the enemy' – an easy enough mistake at night. After refreshing themselves at Skipton they marched on by night, surprising a newly raised troop near Bradford, taking some of them prisoners and the Captain out of his bed, and reached Pomfret whence Colonel Sands was withdrawing on orders from Lord Fairfax in York. Mayney was determined to fight Sands who crossed the Aire by the turnpike at Ferrybridge. 'Our men allights from their horses, takes out of a Smiths Shop a hammer and breaks open the turnpike.' The enemy were waiting to charge them as they were still in the narrow lane, but 'we fight for ground to fight on, fain to seek it thro' gapsteads and places of disadvantage. But having gotten the feild we charged and put them to flight, giving chase to them as far as Sherburn; we took above 50 prisoners.' But Mayney was missing, 'till next day we heard he lay wounded at a town 3 or 4 miles off; and going with a party to fetch him off, we met him coming in a cart; for he had given out, where he lay, that he was of the parliament side, and some soulgiers of the garrison of Pomfret, going out to see what boats they could take upon the river, was told that an officer of the parliament's lay wounded in the town. They were glad of this prize, goes unto him and would have pillaged him, He desired them to take nothing from him in this place, but after they had carried him to Pomfret all he had should be theirs. So they provide a cart for him, being not able to stir by a wound he had in his thigh, and brings him away with a great deal of joy. But they were amazed when we met them; and when he was known, there was much joy that he was returned.' But there was more strife over another prize taken the day before – '13 packs of cloath going to York. They could not agree who should be the sharers with them, whether only the officers of horse, or the garrison to be sharers too.' The captors locked it up in a house and mounted a guard over it, 'which bred so much difference as they were all ready to go together by the eares.' The matter was finally settled by letting everyone have a share, but the captors a double share.

Though the problem of the plundered cloth had been solved that of the Gentlemen in Pomfret was not. They were 'advised what was for their entertainment if they stayed,' but the prospects did not please them for, though Sir Thomas Fairfax was still recovering, in his York house, from the severe wound he had sustained at Helmsley Castle, his father was preparing to come out of York and fight. So they resolved to march to Newark, and Mayney sent his regiment of horse with them, being still confined to bed. Slingsby also stayed behind and was offered command of 'at least 80 Officers and Gentlemen that came for shelter' who, with their servants, 'made a fair Troop. But in the end they could not agree, some being for one and some for another.' When, after eight weeks, Mayney was able to move, the party left for Newark and, by marching by night, arrived unscathed. Here they stayed a fortnight while Mayney's regiment was rehorsed and then set off for Oxford in a smaller party, 'forty one of all sorts. And because our way lay thro' the enemys quarters we provide us a guide and took the night time to march in.' Their first guide took them to Lady Golding's at Colston-Bassett, 15 miles from Newark; and another guide was to lead them to the house of Sir Francis Englefield, whose recusant mother old Sir Henry had once tried to convert – but with no more luck than this guide had when he went ahead to reconnoitre, and did not return. So another guide went, with Slingsby to keep an eye on him, and both got lost in the dark till they found a third man who knew the way. This delay was to cost them dear, for they were still on the march when dawn broke and were sighted by a party of horse from Leicester who rode off to report. They marched on, 'but not with that order as ought to have been in a country where the enemy lay round about us; for we had in our company soulgiers so unruly that they gave the whole country an alarum against us. They would ride out on every hand, take the enemy's horses out of their teams, rob the carryers and play such pranks as we could expect no less than to be mett with by the enemy; and so it fell out.' Near Daventry they were told by a countryman that a troop of horse was just ahead of them. 'We advised for the best,' says Slingsby, 'and yet Sir John Mayney and my Lord St. Paul would by no means we should decline, but march directly by the town. When we were gone a little beyond the town, upon an ascending hill by a woodside we espied their scouts coming forth. Upon the top of the hill, under the woodside, we made a stand and sends before our wearied baggage horse. As soon as they come up towards us we charged them and as fast down again they run. Here we stay not, but after our baggage horse we go, and thus making many haults, gave the enemy time to bring up their whole Troop, and left us no hope but in making the best shift we could to escape. Some of our company had forsaken their horses and betaken themselves to the wood, others followed on as long as they could, and still as they dropt off was taken by the enemy. My man, Thomas Adamson, was once taken, but yet escaped. Tho' I lost all I had, yet had my loss not been so great if Sir John Mayney had not been taken. Altho' afterwards sore wounded at Daintry, my Lord Northampton with a party of horse fetched him off. We were 15 that got to Banbury, and there were 15 taken prisoners; the rest killed, or got away by the darkness of the night. The horse I rid on tyred also, and had it not been for my Lord St. Paul that took me behind him, I had likewise been left behind . . . This day proved of much observation to me, for this same day of the month my father parted with his life and all he had; I also parted with all I had, and in some hazard of my life too, which I shall remember being upon the 17th of December, 1644.' Among the prisoners were Sir John Fenwick who, an old hand at picking winners, soon changed sides. Slingsby stayed in Banbury till Mayney, who had been captured and badly cut about the head, face and neck, was brought in and placed in the care of a doctor. He reached Oxford by Christmas and was lodged 'with great ease and much content' in New Inn Hall with Sir William Parkhurst, the Master of the Royal Mint, who got his medallist, Thomas Rawlins, to strike three medals, to commemorate the march, one for each of Slingsby's children – for Thomas in silver-gilt, for Henry and Barbara in silver. On the medal he is shown a half-length figure with long hair and in steel cuirass, encircled by an inscription 'An earnest Penny for my Children Tho: H. B.: B: Slingsby Oxon 1644,' and a line of Latin which, translated, reads 'from the residue of the money plundered near Daintry under the military authority of Pym.' Two of these medals may be seen, and handled, at the British Museum, and the third at Oriel College, together with the Slingsby Cup, made to replace the wine cup also lost. It was carried by him throughout the rest of the war and shows signs of the rough treatment it endured.[4]

In Oxford, as in the wars of this century, men drilled in the college quads and the Meadows, marched to military lectures, messed in college halls and church-paraded in the Cathedral. Each day Slingsby attended a committee of M.P.'s in the Schools to discuss army administration and discipline. By Magdalen Bridge he watched a demonstration of transporting heavy artillery over the river in specially constructed boats. At the house of General Ruthven[5] (now Earl of Brentford, more infirm, very deaf and no longer so impervious to his liquor after a head wound at the second battle of Newbury) he met Sir Arthur Aston, one-time Governor of the city, who stumped the streets on his wooden leg saying he was 'now able to do cervice with one legge as ever he had been'[6] and, when his successor, Sir Henry Gage, had been killed, asked to be reinstated. But instead Charles appointed, curiously enough, a man called Legge. 'It concerned him,' writes Slingsby, 'to chuse one of trust and care, being for the security of his person, yet he would not transmit all the care to the governour, but would himself once or twice a week take horse and go about the town to view both within and without the works,' It was during Colonel William Legge's governorship that Scrope Metcalfe, Slingsby's nephew and Captain of the Governor's Troop, was mortally wounded leading a raid on parliamentary headquarters at Thame on 6 September, 1645, and died in Oxford.

The king's headquarters were in Christ Church. Here 'he kept his hours most exactly, both for his exercise and for his dispatches, as also his hours for admitting all sorts to come and speak with him. So certain would be his hours, as the sunne's shaddow upon a diall, you might know where he would be at any hour from his rising, which was very early, to his walk he took in the garden, and so to chapple and dinner; so after dinner, if he went not abroad, he had his hours for wryghting or discoursing, or chess playing or tennis.'

At the end of 1644 came 'the great treaty at Uxbridge, great in expectation, tho' in conclusion it brought forth nothing that gave any hopes of peace but rather gave either side warning to prepare the sooner for battle . . . Nothing was expected now but new warr for a new summer, and a new modell of the army for their new-made General Sir Thomas Fairfax', already in training, in their scarlet coats, at Windsor. 'The King, now making all the speed he could to take the field before the parliament forces could be ready,' marched out of Oxford, with the princes Maurice and Rupert, in May of 1645 and, with an army now totalling 5,000 foot and 6,000 horse, made for Evesham. On the way there Rupert ordered the evacuation of Camden House and Slingsby was given the distasteful task of setting it on fire 'lest the enemy should make use of it for a garison . . . a house my Lord Camden says cost £30,000 in building and furniture.'

Reaching Burton-on-Trent, captured by Colonel Marmaduke Darcy on his march south with the Queen, they quartered. The Northern Horse were cheered with the hope that once 'northside of Trent' they would continue marching north. 'Yet they are not much inquisitive, and hitherto shewed a mind indifferent what way they went so they followed their General [Langdale]; and such an army had Caesar of whom they write that he would be so severe and precise in exacting discipline, as he would not give them warning of the time either of journey or battle, but kept them ready, intentive and prest to be led forth upon a sudden every minute of an hour whither soever he would. And as Julius Caesar was severe in requiring an exact observance of strict discipline, so he [Langdale] would teach them to endure hardships by his own example, lighting from his horse and leading them on foot many times with the head bare, whether the sun did shine or the clouds did pour down rain; and in this the King did shew the like, for no weather so foule soever did ever fource him to take his coach, but would shew the like patience in enduring as any of the rest.' From Burton they marched to within 4 miles of Leicester, where 'our scouts gives us warning of some horse that were within half a mile of us where we lay, and greyhounds with them a coursing; Sir Marmaduke sends some horse towards them, and as they advanced we perceived more horse coming from beyond the hill, and still as we drew out more horse towards them, so did they, till they at last appear before us in three bodys. We advance to charge them, and still as we advance they drew orderly off in the rear, keeping still in one body facing us. Thus, sometimes retreating and sometimes making a stand, we fourced them under the works of Leister, and our horse takes the hill which lyeth above the town. From hence we send to the King to give him notice where we were and where we lay that night. The next night, 30 May, the King comes with the rest of the army and begirts the town.' Six guns were mounted, which breached the wall, but the main attack was postponed till midnight, 'the warning to be given to fall on on every side was upon the shooting of six guns; every one had their places set, how one should second another both horse and foot, and Sir Marmaduke Langdale had the reserve.' The breach was bloodily contested but parties with scaling ladders at the lower end of the town were more successful, 'gets over the works, breaks the chain and letts down the drawbridge and fells down the works in two or three several places that our horse may enter, so that by the time it was light the town was ours and the King was carryed on the outside of the town by their works; as he went along, the Committee, who were taken prisoners, puts up their heads and puts off their hats, shewing some obeysance; and the soulgiers would call to the King to shew him where such and such an officer lay dead upon the ground, giving some testimony of his worth and gallantry.' On the Sunday the king ordered a service and sermon in the mayor's church 'but the Mayor had a foul disaster happened to him; for when he should have given his attendance upon the King his mace was plundered from him.'

More serious news was that Fairfax was now besieging Oxford, 'which turned the King's thoughts how to deliver it.' But the northerners needed all his and Langdale's powers of persuasion to induce them to march back to Daventry. In the meantime Fairfax had abandoned the siege and was now only 5 miles from the royalist army who were resting while the king hunted in Fawley Park. The news of the proximity of Fairfax's army, which outnumbered the royal army, caused the king to 'march back again to Harborrow, and in our march we understood that General Fairfax followed with his army upon the side of us 6 miles distant.' He was hoping to be joined by Cromwell, and Rupert strongly urged the king to avoid battle and continue the march north. But he was overruled by Digby and Ashburnham, who thirsted for victory and a return to Oxford. On the very night this disastrous decision was taken Cromwell had joined Fairfax.

On the morning of 14 June 1645 the royal army marched out of Harborough and occupied a hill whence 'we could discern the enemy's horse upon another hill about a mile or two before us, which was the same on which Naseby stood; here we made an hault, but after prayers being said, Prince Rupert draws forth a good body of horse and advanceth towards the enemy where he sees their horse marching up on the side of the hill . . . but being hindered of any nearer approach by reason the place between us was full of burts and water, we wheeled about and by our guides were brought upon a fair peice of ground partly corn, partly heath, under Naseby, about half a mile distant from the place.' Rupert drew up his horse 'in sight of the enemy who were not come to the top of the hill, and begin to draw down their regiments upon the side of the hill . . . He immediately sends to the King to hasten away the foot and cannon, which were not yet come off the hill where they first made the randezvous ; and he perceived that General Fairfax intended not to quitt the advantage of the hill where he had drawn up his men ; so advantageous was it that they could easily observe in what body we drew up our men, whereas they lay without our sight, having the hill to cover them . . . Besides they possessed an hedge upon our right wing which they lined with musqueteers to gall our horse, (as indeed they did) before we could come up to charge theirs. It fell upon prince Rupert to charge at that disadvantage, and many of the Regiment were wounded by shot from the hedge before we could join with theirs on that wing. But he so behaved himself in the charge that he beat them up upon that wing beyond the Hills, and had our success been the like upon our left wing, in probability we might have had the day.' Slingsby was with Langdale and the Northern Horse on the left wing, heavily out-numbered by the enemy. 'But being outfronted and overpoured by their assailants, after they were close joyned, they stood a pritty while, and neither seemed to yeild, till more came up to their flanks and put them to rout, and wheeling to our right took them in disorder and so presently made our whole horse run ; and our foot thus left naked were fourced to lay down their arms.' They rallied and joined Rupert's horse for a second charge, 'but we could not abide it, they being horse and foot in good order and we but a few horse only, and those mightily discouraged ; so that we were immediately made to run, and the enemy in pursuit of us gained bag and baggage which they found to be a very rich pillage. And tho' our waggons were left at a good distance yet could they not be carryed off, but some were taken, and some over-thrown and monys shaken out, which made our soulgiers to venture their lives once more, which was but to stay and take it up. The way I took was upon my right hand, leaving

THE
LORIOVS AND
MIRACVLVOS
BATTELL AT YORK.

*This Letter beeing directed to a Noble and honourable
Lord, from the Scots Leaguer lying at York.*

MY LORD,

THese are to give your Lordship accompt of the victorie. It hath pleased G O D to bestow on us far above
our deserts. The way was thus, Prince *Rupert* advancing for *York*, we brake up our beligering to meet him,
having an order (which wee intercepted) from the
, that nothing but impossibilities should stay him from beating
cots: As we were marching, he put the River of *Ewes* betwixt us,
at he came to *York* without any stop, so that we lay foure myles
-from, and on the morrow brake up the march to *Todcaster* to
d his retreate.

Foot having the way, we were not one myle from it, the Alarme
sent us by our Horse, that Prince *Rupert* was with his whole
advancing, which made us presently march back to the bounds
ad left, where we found him drawing up in a plaine field three
es of length and breadth; the fairer for such use I had not seene
ngland, we finding him so neer. and no possibilitie to have our
n two houres, keeped the advantage of a sleeke, and the hills
our Horse, till the Foot as they came up was put in order: In
meane time wee advanced our Canon, and entred to play on
a on the left wing, which made them a little to move, with it they
eiving, brought up theirs, and gave us the like. This continued
ong, when it was resolved wee should advance downe the hill
a great field of corne, to a ditch they had in possession,
t it pleased God so to prosper, they were put from i, so that
service went on verie hote on all sides : We losing on the right
g, and gaining on the left, they that fought stood extraordinar
to it; whereof my Lord *Lindesays* Briggad beeing commanded
imself, was one. These Briggads that tailyied of the Vane were
ently supplied by *Cassels*, *Comper*, *Dumfermling*, and some of
isdailes Regiment, who were on the battell, and gained what they
loft. and made themselves master of the Canon was next to them,
rooke Sir *Charles Lewcas* Leivetenant Generall of their Horse
ner : These that ran away shew themselves most basely. I com-
ding the Battel, was on the head of your Lordships Regiment and
euches, but they carried themselves not so as I could have wished,
her could I prevaile with them : For these that fled, never came to
ge with the enemie, but were so possest with a panatick feare, that
ran for an example to others, and no enemie following them,
ch gave the enemie to charge them, they intended not, & they had
the losse. These that fought, God preserved them miraculously
no losse, we have only the Lord *Dudup* prisoner, and Lievete-
Collonel *Brison* is killed, two Captaines, and some Souldiers:
have Sir *Charles Lewcas*, Generall Major *Porter*, some Collo-
, and other officers, with sundrie of their chiefe Officers killed
: number killed to the enemie as is estimate, is two thousand, and
we, with fifteene hundreth prisoners, twentie piece of Canon,

which was all they had, all their Amonition, all their Baggage, ten
thousand armes, all their foot Colours, many Cornets, the horse
on the right winge were beat: My Lord *Eglingtown* not being well seconded, Sir *Thomas Fairfax* commanded there in chief, a brave Commander, but his horse answered not our expectation nor his worth,
they gave some blame to the commanded Muscariers that were with
him: My Lord *Eglingtown* commanded our horse there, who shewed himselfe most valiantly, his Son relieving his father, who was far
ingagded, is sore wounded, our left wing of horse, which was commanded by Lievetenant Generall *Cromwel*, and General Major *David
Leslie* caried themselves bravely, and under God was a maine occasion of our victorie. I must not overpasse *Manchesters* Foot, who did
good service under the command of Generall Major *Cransurd*; Our
Generall being chief Commander himself, Lievetenant Generall *Baillie* commanded the Vane of ours under him, so *Fairfax* and *Manchester* of their own. So not troubling your Lordship further, I rest.

*At our Leigour at York, the
fifth of July, 1 6 4 4.*

*Heere is another Letter written by a trustie Gentle
man, to another Noble and honourable
Lord, in the Kingdome of Scotland.*

MY LORD,

AT our comming before *Yorke* yesterday, the Towne was
summoned to render to our Generall by a Trumpeter; wee
had this day a fair answere from Sir *Thomas Glenning*, and
the Mair of the Citie Master *Cowper*, which was neither a grant, nor
a refusall : But we hope since the Prince hath left them, with a small
bodie of horse, and our whole Caviliers in in pursute of him, and
that the Message of N.... with our Countrey-man *King*, and all
their good Officers are gone: They will shortly accep. of quarters,
for as we understand, and by certaine intelligencies from the Towne
this day, they have not five hundred Souldiers in the Town, beside the
traine Bands, and the Burgars : So if they render not upon quarters
which wee heartily wish to prevent more bloud, wee intend by Gods
asistance, to take it by storme : Wee were cer..ly informed from
one which came out of the Towne this day, That the Prince brought
scarce in with him to the towne of his Foot (confessed by Sir Charles Lewcas to be twelve thousand) not five hundreth, but were either killed, or run away: The Papists and Bishops, and their com-
plices have all left the Town, Bag and Baggade: The greatest losse we
hive was the spoiling of our Biggadge, and horse, most of the
battell, by our owne men that fled, and our Baggadge, some our losses are estimed to be in horse, money and clothes, above twoo scorenoreth
thousand pounds Scots : I hope some of it shall be recoverd. I am
losser my selfe above three thousand merkes, and Sir *James Lumbis-
din* two thousand. But we heartily dispence with the losse of meanes,
since God hath prospered the worke in our hands, I hope by Gods
blessing, this blow the Prince hath gotten shall bee a good meanes to
bring all the businesse here to a good happie close, to Gods glorie,
(to whom only the praise of the worke is due) and the good of the
three Kingdomes.

This battell was fought on twesday the second of *July*; a day
ought never to be forgot in the three Kingdomes, as one of the greatest
acts of Gods great power and mercie manifested to us, for which
we have a solemne thankesgiving the next Lords day : And as it is
expected in all the Kingdomes will be the like, so soone as can be ex-
pediently.

---

*Gentle Reader, I crave your Patience concerning the drawing up of the Briggads, because they were not altogether so perfet
as I would have them : But yee shall have them very shortly God willing printed in a perfect forme.*

Printed at E D I N B V R G H by James Lindesay, 1 6 4 4.

This is the broadside mentioned on p. 76. Both the letters are unsigned and the spelling
was anglicised, as comparison with the transcription of the original in Appendix 179–81,
will show.   *(By permission of the National Library, Edinburgh.)*

The silver Slingsby Cup and Medal, in the Library of Oriel College, Oxford, described on pp. 88 & 93.　　　　　　　　　　　(*by permission of the Provost and Fellows of Oriel College*)

Harborrow on my left, only Leif. Coll Atkinson and three more following me when all ours besides took Harborrow on the right and were come to Leister long before we got thither.' Slingsby's line was a good 20 miles over rolling country now hunted, with less risk to life and limb, by the Pytcheley and Fernie. Monckton 'staide with the last in the field,' having three horses shot under him. He was chased for 10 miles but managed to bring his prisoner, a Captain, to Leister.[7] Digby who, as amateur soldier, had advised the king to fight, failed as Secretary of State, to secure the king's cabinet full of his private correspondence which, by its indiscretions, shocked his friends and delighted his enemies.[8] In addition Charles lost all his infantry and guns and, three days later, Leicester with its magazine. The royal cause never recovered from this disaster.

1   See West, 'Antiquities of Furness', for account of the Prestons.
2   Clarendon IX, 2.
3   D. Lloyd, Memoirs of Excellent Personages.
4   There is a double connection between the Slingsbys and Oriel. Sir Thomas Slingsby married Dorothy Cradock, grand-daughter of Dr. John Saunders who had been Provost of Oriel from 1644 till his death in 1653; and the Rev. Daniel Parsons, who edited and published the Diary in 1836, was also an Oriel man. It was the late F. J. Varley, Hon. Fellow of Oriel, who bought the medal and cup from an Oxford jeweller in 1943 and presented them to the College.
5   His portrait today hangs in the Bodleian.
6   In a fall, 'kerveting on horseback' before some ladies, he broke his leg, which later had to be amputated. But in 1646 he was serving under Ormond in Ireland and in 1649 was in command at Drogheda where he repulsed Cromwell's first assault, but in the storming of the city he was 'hewn in pieces and his brains dashed out with his wooden leg'. Anthony Wood's Diary (quoted by F. J. Varley in 'Oxford in the Civil War).
7   Monckton Papers, 19.
8   C. V. Wedgwood, 'The King's War'.

Chapter ten

1645 – 1646

AFTER NASEBY the royalist army moved west to Lichfield, then south to the safety of Hereford, 'cituated not much unlike to York . . . for it hath a round tower mounted upon a hill like to Clifford's Tower, and the river Wye running close to it.' Thence on to Raglan where the king and some of the lords stayed three weeks in the castle as guests of the octogenarian Earl of Worcester, 'and passed their time much in bowling' on the spacious bowling green much admired by Charles for its views to the west. Here 'the King omitted not his accustomed hours for prayers, according to the form of the Church of England, and in that house where never before any form was used [Worcester being a Roman Catholic] and on Tuesday he would have his sermon, as usually he had at Whitehall, in the parish church a quarter of a mile off, brought thither in his coach.' He would have heard more home truths than in the sermon from his out-spoken host, on those visits he paid him after dinner, who 'read the King such a lesson that all the standers-by were amazed at his boldness.'[1]

Charles was now planning to make Bristol his head-quarters, and Rupert crossed the Severn one night to meet him 'at Mr. Moore's house, a little distant from the black rock' [Blackrock today] and discuss the plan. But the fall of Bridgwater put an end to this. Still hoping to raise an army in South Wales he visited all the garrisons. At Cardiff he once more met Archbishop Ussher,[2] the Governor's father-in-law, the man who had implored him not to sacrifice

94

Strafford, and had taken his last message to this devoted servant as he lay in the Tower, a memory that haunted Charles to the day of his own execution – as well it might. When it was clear that little help was forthcoming in South Wales Charles decided to go north and try to join up with Montrose in Scotland. The royal army reached Doncaster, where reports of Sydenham Poyntz's army further north and the Scottish Horse coming up from the south, caused it to turn back to Newark; thence on to Stamford where a captured Scots major said 'he could easily have beaten up our quarters and taken the King if he could have had any confidence in his men, who were new raised.' From Stamford they advanced into Cromwell country and surprised the garrison of Huntingdon. The town was plundered and the troops rearmed themselves. Among papers found was a list of those who had signed the Covenant, and a letter showing 'how many people were adicted to idolise the King, with many quotations and texts out of Scripture.' Turning south west for Oxford they next quartered at Woburn, 'my Lord of Bedford's house, without great interruption,' and at Wing where a soldier was hanged from a sign post for stealing a chalice from a church, the only severity Slingsby observed in the king 'either toward the enemy when he had him in his power, or to the soulgier in the army.' At Oxford the king 'tarryed but one day, not knowing where to repose himself, and yet wheresoever he marched he was sure enough to be followed by Poyntz, who had his orders given him to attend the King's motion. Therefore the King will once again secure himself among the mountains of Wales, but first he will go to relieve the siege of Hereford.'

So the round tour began once more: first to Worcester, then Hereford where 'the people were joyfull of the King's coming and many came out to meet him,' and then on to Raglan, crossing the Wye by a wooden bridge built by the Scots, which so caught Slingsby's imagination that he gives a detailed description of its construction, likening it to the wooden bridge built over the Rhine by Caesar, whose description he quotes in full. At Raglan the fateful news of Rupert's surrender of Bristol on 10 September reached the king, and he dashed off a furious letter to his nephew, banishing him from the country. Among the garrison, who had been allowed to march out with flying colours, were two of Slingsby's cousins, Captain Robert Slingsby, the sailor who had raised a regiment of seamen during the siege,[3] and his brother Colonel Walter Slingsby who had commanded the Great Fort[4] and was to fight on to the bitter end in the siege of Pendennis Castle.

Raglan was no longer safe and the king's only hope seemed to lie, as before, in the north. Poyntz was still hot on his heels but the royal army eluded him, marching 'thro' the almost unaccessable mountains of Wales.' Accommodation was rough, and the best they found was at Old Radnor 'where the King lay in a poor low chamber, and my Lord of Lindsey and others by the kitching fire on hay; no better were we accommodated for victuals, which makes me remember this passage. When the King was at his supper eating a pullet and a peice of cheese, the room without was full, but the men's stomachs empty for want of meat; the good wife, troubled with continual calling upon her for victuals and having, it seems, but that one cheese, comes into the room where the King was, and very soberly asks if the King had done with the cheese for the gentleman without desired it. But the best was we never tarryed long in any place, and therefore might the more willingly endure one night's hardship, in hopes the next night might be better.' They made for Chester in an attempt to relieve it, for it was the chief port for Ireland and the Irish army Charles was still expecting, and entered it from the Welsh unguarded side. Langdale, sent out to drive the besiegers off, was caught by Poyntz and forced off Rowton Heath with heavy losses by Colonel Hugh Bethell, who himself lost an eye. Among the dead was the king's cousin and commander of his Lifeguard, Lord Bernard Stuart, 'whom he loved so dearly.' Charles had watched the defeat of his cavalry from the walls. 'Here I do wonder at the admirable temper of the King,' comments Slingsby, 'whose constancy was such that no perills, never so unavoidable, could move him to astonishment; but that still he set the same face and settled countenance upon what adverse fortune soever befell him; and neither was exalted in prosperity nor dejected in adversity; which was the more admirable in him, seeing he had no other to have recourse unto for councell and assistance but must bear the whole burden upon his shoulders. But this makes him look the nearer to his own safety, and therefore gives orders for his march the next day with those horse that came safe to the town.' They marched to the security of Denbigh Castle to reorganise and, shortly afterwards, retraced their steps, making cross-country 'by unknown ways and passages, with many dark and late marches,' for Newark. Here the plan to reach Scotland and Montrose was still favoured by the king, but Montrose's retreat to the highlands, after the defeat of his Irish troops at Philiphaugh, and his appeal for reinforcements, made it unsafe. But Langdale and the Northern Horse, now under the command of George, Lord Digby, set off for the north, only to get the worst of a fight at Sherburn in which Sir Richard Hutton was killed and Robert Slingsby lost his right hand and was left for dead.

Newark was still safe, and of great strategic importance situated as it was at the crossing of the Trent by the Great North Road from Newcastle and York, and the Foss Way from Lincoln, and so could keep open the route from the north to Leicester, Nottingham and the royalist head-quarters at Oxford. It was while Charles was here in October that Rupert stormed into the royal presence to defend his surrender of Bristol and demand a court-martial; and that the subsequent 'mutiny' of senior officers took place, and Sir Richard Willys, one of Rupert's friends, was removed from the Governorship and replaced by John (now Lord) Belasyse. Slingsby did not witness these dramatic events for he had gone to Redhouse to get money 'whereof a long time I had great scarcity.' And before he returned the king had gone to Oxford – a hunted man, riding fast and doing the journey in two days. Since he left it seven months before he had marched, with his army, nearly 1,500 miles. Slingsby in the meantime went first to Hazelwood, the Vavasour home whose owner, Sir Walter, was in exile having lost one brother at Marston Moor and another at Tewkesbury. 'I tarryed about a month at Hazelwood and kept in so privately that I was not seen of any. And I went to my own house; I took the night time for it, and in the night I returned, scarce any in my own house knowing that I was there.' Cross-country it is 12 miles from Hazelwood to Redhouse and the way lay over Marston Moor, still littered with grim relics of the battle. Slingsby's thoughts, as he rode that way alone to his own home filled with memories he had tried to forget, with the knowledge that the royal cause was all but lost, must have been sombre as the night. Staying one night at Redhouse and taking £40 in gold, he returned to Newark – 'and that must be presently, for the Scots had appointed a randezvous in order to their march to Newark, and I must not think to go thither if I got not thither before them; and as I came, so I went, in disguise, but not the same way; for I came by Doncaster, but I went back by Cowick through the Levell, and by good fortune returned safe to Newark.'

He beat the Scots to Muskham Bridge, which soon after they seized because the royalist guard retreated before the fire lit to destroy it had taken hold. This enabled the Scots to come within the Isle and bring their artillery up. Belasyse had been organising the defences and strengthening the outer ditch with pitfalls – 'two rows of holes the height of a man in depth.' He saw to it that every man knew his action stations and he coninued to harass the enemy by sending out fighting patrols 'which put them to so hard duty in so cold and frosty a winter as was not almost to be endured.' The ice was thick enough for horse and foot to fight on it. But a more deadly foe, the plague, penetrated the defences and infected houses had to be shut up and guarded. By the end of March 1646 there were 16,000 Scots and English troops investing Newark at musket-shot range and Belasyse was summoned to surrender. 'Now all hopes of releife was taken from us,' writes Slingsby. 'We could not rely anything upon the King, for he was close besieged at Oxford; neither could we expect any relief from the Marquis of Montross, for Davie Leslie had chased him into the mountains; yet we had provision enough to hold out yet longer.'

The next report they had was from the Scottish camp where 'the King was come among them in disguise, willing rather to yeild himself unto the Scots, who shewed some moderation, than to the parliament of England who so vehemently persecuted him. Therefore he sends to the Governour to make up an agreement speedily.' These orders, as Belasyse told Pepys at dinner 20 years later, and Pepys retold, were 'sent in a slugge bullet, being wryt in cypher, wrapt up in lead and swallowed. So the messenger came to my Lord and told him he had a message from the King but it was yet in his belly. So they did give him some physique and out it did come.'⁵ Belasyse, through the commissioners he appointed (who included his brother Henry), made the best terms he could and the garrison of 2,000, so over-officered that there were more than twenty four colonels, marched out on 8 May, 1646.⁶

Slingsby now 'took the opportunity of having the company of a Scotch Captain who came to view the garrison a day before we yeilded up the town ; and so lay that night at Kelham at Mrs. Love's house where the King had lodged the night before.' They joined the Scottish army, with the king, at Tuxford and marched north with them. Slingsby admired their good discipline, 'both in taking up their quarters and in their march. Whether it was by reason of the King being with them or that was usual for them to do I cannot tell ; but they shewed a great deal of celerity ; not a man scarce seen to be straggling or be out of rank, and if they made an hault they never made it both with horse and foot together ; but if the horse haulted the foot marched through. A little before we came to Topcliffe, where the King dined, I was commanded by the King to return home ; which was, as I said before, upon the 11th of May 1646.' He went first to Newburgh where his 13-year-old daughter was, and then on to Redhouse, an event commemorated by Adamson who, 'at my homecoming set that ash which grows by the causeway as you go by the cowstables to the Ings.'

1 Charles Heath, 'History and Description of Raglan Castle', 86.
2 It was Archbishop Ussher who, in his 'Annals of the World. etc.' of 1658, wrote: 'I encline to this opinion, that from the evening ushering in the

first day of the world, to that midnight which began the first day of the Christian era, there were 4003 years, 70 days and 6 temporarie howers', and that Man was created on Friday, 28th October.

3 Hollond, 'Discourses of the Navy', lxxviii. HMC XI Report, App. vii, 40.
4 Rawl MS, A 61, p. 35.
5 Pepys, 4 February, 1665.
6 There is a marginal correction to 7 May in Slingsby's handwriting.

Chapter eleven

1646 – 1652

BUT IT WAS NO PEACEFUL HOME-COMING. 'I had not been here above a month's space but, contrary to their faith given and Articles of Rendition of Newark, the Mayor Alderman Watson sends soulgiers to apprehend me; but having a little notice given of their intention I slipt out of their way and for a long time kept so close within my house that they could never tell where I was. I betake myself to one room scarce known to my servants, where I spend my days in great sylence, scarce dare to speak or walk but with great heed lest I be discovered. This gave me liberty of being out of their hands, but deprived me of my health, as wanting liberty to enjoy the fresh air, and keeping close in one room without air did stifle the vital spirits, and meeting with a crazy body made so by the immoderate bleeding of the hemorrhoides, with excess of humours through want of exercise, did so distemper all the parts that, unless by the help of a glyster, I could never go to the stool. The time when this disease first appeared was about the year 1626, which caused me to seek advice from Dr. Leake, not knowing then what it might be. And he as ignorantly would have it to proceed from a weakness in the liver, and applied his cure accordingly. But time hath given me more experience, since from that time it never left me and in future will bring me to my grave.'

This lonely incarceration, 'as bad as an imprisonment,' after years of active service in the company of friends, must have been hard to endure. The Articles of Newark should have given him three months peace, but already they were trying to make him take the Negative Oath and the National Covenant – 'the one makes me renounce my alegiance and the other my religion . . . Why should the oath not to assist the King, being contrary to former oaths we have taken, be imposed when all means is taken from us whereby we might assist him?[1] As for the Covenant they would have me take there is first reason that I should be convinced of the lawfulness of it before I take it and not urged, as the Mahometans do their disciples, by fource and not by reason . . . For by this new religion which is imposed you make every man that takes it up guilty either of having no religion or else a religion put off and on, as he doth his hat to every one he meets. See how impartial you are, for when in former times it was thought greivous that conformity should be imposed by the bishops (when the scruple should be only a cap or a sirplice) you scrupled at the out branches only, but we scruple to have root and branch plucked up; therefore judge of our scruple by your own. It makes me remember that riddle of the water and the ice: *Mater me genuit, eadem mox gignitur ex me*, We once got you, but now you get us. God keep us out of your hands!'

Most royalists took the two oaths 'for quietness sake.' In the words of the topical song:

"They force us to take
Two oaths, but we'll make
A third, that we ne'er meant to keep 'em."

Slingsby took neither, and so was unable to compound and save his estates from the threat of confiscation. Clarendon says 'he remained still in his own house, prepared and disposed to run the fortune of the Crown in any other attempt; and having a good fortune and a general reputation, had a greater influence upon the people than they who talked more and louder; and was known to be irreconcileable to the new government.'

One can imagine some of the things that were said, and were to be repeated *ad nauseam* by those of his relations who had made their peace, about this ridiculous attitude. One result of this close confinement, however, was to give us the second part of the Diary, which begins: 'Here I will leave the Armie to tell my own story, where I have been ever since I marched out of York, July 1644 untill the 7th of May, 1646; for I have now good leisure in the solitariness wherein I live; and the setting down the places and times wherein I spent my two yeares' peregrination, and the taking a revew thereof will serve to put off the tediousness of my close retirement.' His account of those two years has already been summarised and only the last few pages remain, which tell how parliament, then dominated by his cousin Sir Philip Stapylton and Denzil Holles, 'treated with the Scots to have the King returned back to them, making shew they would give him an honourable reception, and to perswade the more they make ready for his entertainment Holmby House: and to give better colour to their feigned friendship they send my Lord Pembroke, once his Lord Chamberlain, to receive him and conduct him to Holmby.' With him went Northumberland. 'The Scots were easily perswaded to deliver him, and dismissed the forces they had prepared, and then the parliament with great modesty requests a place of meeting, to end all controversies by conference; to all which the King yeilds, with a facility of nature, and the parliament accepts of all with a reserved meaning, untill having gott him into the house appointed for his entertainment they made him at last known he was their prisoner.' Pembroke and Northumberland, the wyvern and the lion on that staircase of friends and brothers, had played their part, little knowing what it would lead to. 'While I remained concealed in my own house,' Slingsby continues, 'I could hear of his going to Holmby, to the Isle of Weight, and to Whitehall at last, where he ended his good life upon the 30th of January 1648/9, I hear. *Heu me: quid heu me? Inhumana perpessi sumus*. Thus I have ended these commentaries or book of rememberance, beginning in the year 1638 and ending in the year 1648.'

Not quite ended for there is still half a page on the natural phenomena that marked these two dates: the gales of 1638 with which the Diary opened, 'as I took notice in the beginning of this book;' and the great floods of 1648, when it rained from the beginning of May till mid-September, which marked 'a year fatal and very remarkable, in which the Scots lost their army, and the English their King, and to stand as a perpetual mark, the same flood that carryed down the root of a tree with the volume of it, like to Root and Branch, leaves it upon the bank of the West Ings at Redhouse. *Elevarunt flumina fluctus suos, et conturbaverunt eum.*'

Though the Diary was ended the story of its author was not. He continued to correspond with his old comrades in arms, Langdale and Mayney. Langdale had been in exile abroad since his vain efforts to join Montrose in Scotland. But he was said to have crossed to visit the King, in disguise, at Hampton Court, and certainly did so to lead the northern rising of 1648. It was on his way with forces from the north to relieve Colchester that he wrote encouragingly to Sir Charles Lucas 'Dear Sir, hold out but a little, a very little space; your friends will visit you, and bring you off with honour,'[2] a feat he was confident of achieving till he met Cromwell's army near Preston and was defeated in a desperate battle. Soon after this he was captured and imprisoned in Nottingham Castle. He wrote from here to Slingsby, giving what he called 'a just accompt of my last imployment,' a detailed description of events leading up to the battle and of the battle itself of which he says : 'If I had had a 1000 men to have flancked the enemy I doubt not but the day had bin ours.'[3] This letter could hardly have reached Redhouse before he made his escape from the castle, aided by Lady Savile, Sir William's gallant widow. First he reached his cousin's house at Houghton disguised as a parliamentary soldier; thence, dressed up as a milkmaid in print gown and sun-bonnet, riding one of the cows out to pasture (as was the local custom) he went to ground in a stone-pit for some days; from here he reached and swam the Humber and journeyed on, impersonating a clergyman, to London and overseas – all with a high price on his head.[4]

The next year Sir John Mayney wrote to cheer Slingsby up with the news that, only six weeks after Charles I's execution his son, 'our most hopefull King is received at Brussels with huge galantries, and intends (by the way of France) for Dublin which will be ready for his Coorte in peace about 20 days hence, God willing.' God was not willing, but this letter from an old friend, which ends 'If trowbles arise neere you, let my Cottage bee happy with your presence, and doubt not but I shall serve you with that fidelity as becomes your moste Reall affectionate faythfull servant J. M.,' must have warmed Slingsby's heart.[5] Mayney had been fined twice, £1,600 in March and again £1,970 in August, for his part in a royalist rising in 1648 on Charles II's birthday, 29 May, in which he had held Maidstone with 2,000 men against an army of 10,000 commanded by Fairfax who described the street by street resistance as more desperate than any he had yet encountered.[6] These fines ruined him and he had to sell his home, sunny Linton Place overlooking the Weald.[7] His neighbour, Sir George Sandes, of Throwley, where Slingsby had waited with Preston years before, had already compounded for £30,000 and been imprisoned in the Tower; now, when his estates were sequestered, he had to fell his woods to pay further fines.[8]

News would have reached Slingsby of his cousins, the three brothers, Arthur, Robert and Walter. Arthur, late a Colonel of Horse, had escaped to France 'in a shallop' hard on the heels of the sea-sick John Evelyn,[9] and was now secretary to the Earl of Bristol who was pressing the Spanish alliance. Robert is said to have joined him after recovering from his wound and, like Langdale, crossed the channel now and then in disguise to visit Charles I in captivity, being employed by him 'on his most private negotiations, for which he was cast into a loathesome dungeon.'[10] Walter, described by one government agent as 'a little man, black hair half turned grey, hath pockholes in his face, a dangerous person,'[11] had also escaped to France from Pendennis Castle but returned to organise a resistance movement in Cornwall where he was captured and sent to the Tower.

Slingsby had his own worries, both about the threatened confiscation of all his estates, and the future of his motherless children, aged 13, 10 and 7, who might innocently give him away whenever the house was searched. This may have been the time when the Latin lines were painted on the blacka-more's post, asking this little black exile – '*Melandre Profugus*'[12] – where in the name of all the gods peace of mind might be found if neither nightfall nor sleep could bring it. Slingsby admits he found 'recreation' in reading and writing and teaching his children. But, unlike most fathers home after war, he was still a hunted man. Maybe this, combined with the long separation, bound the family even more closely together, to stand four-sqaure to the dangers from without.

At the end of 1650 he received a letter from his uncle, Sir Francis, who had lost his estates in Connaught during the rebellion two years before, which may have embarassed him, financially straitened as he was. For Sir Francis first reminds him of the small annuity he had originally received from the family estate, and how he had subsequently 'gone abroad into the world' to better himself and with God's blessing 'attained to a good fortune,' but since he has now lost it he is forced to fly into his nephew's 'armes of compassion.' God has punished him for his sins, he acknowledges his just chastisement, and craves His pardon and reception into His heavenly glory. Working up to the main purpose of the letter he continues, 'You know that this doth not concerne my selfe (whoe could willingly now lay downe my life) but my sonn in lawe, my daughter, and her child, whoe gives some testimony, if he may be kept still at schoole, of inablinge himselfe to some future fortune to advance him heereafter : much more could I say but leave it to God to inspire into your hart and to looke upon the case as it now stands with me. P.S. If God shall please to enable me with something out of Ireland I shall make full compensation of all the favours you have done me.' The son-in-law was a Captain William Dodwell, an Irishman who had married Elizabeth Slingsby. In the year of the Irish rebellion they had brought their son Henry, then aged 7, to be educated in the Free School in York. Dodwell had gone back to Ireland where he died of the plague, and soon after this his wife died too, leaving Henry penniless at school. Slingsby did his best for the boy, inviting him to spend his holidays with his cousins at Redhouse and giving him some of the clothes they had grown out of. Henry more than fulfilled his grandfather's expectations and ultimately became one of the finest theological, historical and classical scholars in Europe. He was also one of those Non-Jurors who had the courage to proclaim their loyalty to the Stuart cause.

As the threat of confiscation drew near, and Slingsby still refused the two oaths, his father-in-law (who had himself compounded to the tune of £5,995) wrote from London, 'Good Son, You are in the greate booke of selling estates, and manie frends your name had when it was voted against you; therefore let not your estate be ruinated, nor your woods felled, but cum up and sollicit it yourselfe, and I am assured by one of your frends that yet it may be saved if you cum in tyme. Once again let me desire you to cum up speedily. I lye at the Golden Still in Holborne.' His nephew the Reverend William Bethell, also implored him 'by all the ties of nature and reason to pitty yourself and children and provide in time the best you can for your safety, which every creature would doe, lest, despising all councell, you fall unpittied of any but your friends whoe then also will be able only to stand staring upon you as Job's friends did, but prove miserable comforters.' His brother-in-law, Brian Stapylton, wrote even more urgently 'the sale of your estate will be most certayne yf not speedily prevented; I pray you therefore signifie your desyres to my nephew Slingsbie Bethell what you would have him doe, and withall by some safe hande send up your evidence to him, whearebie he may be enabled to contracte with the Trustees. Your Sister remembers hir love to you, and joynes with me in this requeste for your owne good.' Slingsby Bethell (Dryden's Shimei 'Whose youth did early promise bring, Of zeal to God and hatred to his King') was probably the last person Slingsby wanted to appeal to but, sinking his pride, he wrote 'Nephew, Your neare relation to me and your interest with the Parliament make me thinke you a fitt meade to meadeate for a mitigation of their severe sentence against me. For I desire to know what on my part is not done which you would have me to do . . . They have called upon me to compound, but how unfitt I am to undertake it you may judge.' He has neither ready money nor credit, being but a tenant for life by strict entail; and he lives under 'three heavy censures which are : exile, ever to remain in one place ;

confiscation ; and *capitis diminutio*, that is a depriving of all power in the least matter to act as a Countryman.'[13] Nevertheless he concludes 'If you will lett me know when it is needfull to send up my deed of entail I shall not faile.'

Slingsby Bethell pledged his own credit and, by borrowing from his brothers and the Stapyltons, managed to buy Redhouse, Moor Monkton and other parts of the estate round Knaresborough for £7,000 and was able to assure his uncle 'Your whole estate is in their hands who will be true and faithfull trustees for you and your children.' But he could not resist adding 'Since it is noe worse, I wish that, tho' it may not worke in you a discovery of the errour of your Judgement, as I must call it, it may at least raise up your owne and all your friends' harts in thankfulness unto God, that he has not at this time determined the ruine of your family, as hee seems to have done by all in your condition, your selfe only excepted.'

He spoke too soon. The Committee for Sequestrations in the City of York sent in demands for rent and refused to answer the Trustees' letters, even when they protested 'Wee remain astonisht to consider that wee, who have hazarded our estates, our lives, our All that was deare to us with the forwardest in contesting against the malignant interest, should now find ourselves aggrieved and attempted to bee wronged by that power which ought to maintaine us in our rights.' But the President of the Committee in York, Major General Lilburne, a tough soldier who had commanded the most mutinous regiment in the parliamentary army[14] and been one of the regicides, would not have been much impressed by any hazards run by the Trustees, especially since he must have suspected what was going on in the country houses all round York. Slingsby might write 'Lett them doe with me what they will, I am resolved by God's grace to live retired and practise to learn that hard lesson in Christianitie, to pray for my enemies,' but he fluug out a challenge in a cryptic inscription, set up over the figure of a setting sun on one of the west walls of Redhouse that reflected those memorable sunsets over the Wood :

> *"Paulisper et Relucebis*
> *Et Ipse, M.R.* 29. 1652"

M.R. almost certainly stands for Meus Rex, my King; 29 was the date of Charles II's birthday; 1652 was the year after Worcester and Charles's flight to France when Royalist hopes were at their lowest. The meaning must have been clear to his confidants : 'In a short time both you [the sun] and he himself, my King, will shine forth again.'

Though some of those whose crests Slingsby had set up on the staircase may have wished the same, none was to prove willing to risk his neck again to achieve it. More than half were dead. First Walter Bethell, long before the war, leaving his widow to bring up their five sons and four daughters. Though puritans and divided in politics they had united to help to save his estates from confiscation. Next to go had been Alice Waterton – 'that incomparable Gentlewoman Mistress Alice, pride of Slyngesby's race, Waterton's glory, who in her progeny illustrious still remains' – as her husband wrote of her in epitaph.[15] The progeny were six daughters and three sons, of whom Thomas had succeeded to Walton Hall which was besieged in the summer of '45 while he was away at the war. His wife held it and evidence of the siege still remains in the musket balls embedded in the stout oak doors,[16] a better fate than that of Sir William Savile's Thornhill, burnt to prevent its use by the enemy. Savile had commanded a regiment of foot and captured Leeds whence he managed to escape, on its recapture, by swimming his horse over the Aire. After this he became Governor of Sheffield, and then York where he died in 1643. But his widow continued the fight, held Sheffield Castle (where she brought forth a son during the bombardment) was probably behind the raid to seize General Rainsborough and exchange him for Langdale, and certainly helped Langdale to escape from Nottingham Castle. The authorities 'laid their snares on all sides to entrap her,' but failed.[17] The Savile owl, which today amuses the beholder, would have held deep memories for Slingsby. Cumberland died in York in the same year as Savile and was buried in Skipton Castle which held out to the end of the war. He was the last of the Cliffords but his sister Ann, came to live there in 1650 on the death of her husband, the Earl of Pembroke, he who had preferred the safety of Wilton to that of the king and had from his room in the Cockpit, watched him walk to his execution.[18] His would not have been a name to sound sweet in Slingsby's ears, any more than Northumberland's who died the same year, after being of little more help to the king than to care for the royal children while their father was a prisoner in Hampton Court.

Of the brothers-in-law still alive two had lost sons – Scrope Metcalfe at Thame and John Fenwick, 'that excellent horseman,' at Marston Moor.[19] Metcalfe was now nearing his end but Fenwick had, since the war, procured a testimonial from the Standing Committee of Northumberland that 'to the best of their knowledge he had always adhered to the Parliament and not to the King'[20] – a remarkable lapse of memory for this one-time Master General of the Royal Army and Master of the Royal Studs. Sir Walter Vavasour had returned from exile abroad to reclaim his sequestered estates. The Ingrams had suffered fines but little else and father, thrice married, and his two sons lived on in their respective homes. Slingsby's best friends now were the Stapyltons. They had helped to save his estates and Brian had come to see him whenever he could, even when he was in hiding.[21] Both the Stapylton cousins who had been up at Queens' with him were dead, Robert before the war, Philip after a meteoric career in the parliamentary army, and in Parliament as one of its leaders against Cromwell for which he was impeached but escaped to Calais where he died on landing. One good thing he had done, in Slingsby's eyes, was to rescue the royalist President of Queens' from the ship in which he and other Heads of Colleges were battened down for shipment to the slave markets of the West Indies.[22] Old Lord Fauconberg lingered on, a sick man, but Newburgh would now have to go to his grandson for Henry, his eldest son, had died the year after he came back from Newark. John, Lord Belasyse, who had so distinguished himself, and suffered, in the war had returned to Worlaby after surrendering Newark. But finding it plundered he went over-seas. Slingsby would have heard of his doings there – service under the Prince of Condé at the siege of Mardyke, his waiting in readiness to cross to England in '48 and command Newcastle's Horse in Yorkshire, a plan that failed when Langdale was beaten at Preston, and his return in 1650, to be promptly imprisoned in the Tower.[23]

Lastly Fairfax, now Lord Fairfax, who like himself was confined to his home, but by old wounds and gout and a disinclination to have any more to do with a government founded on blood. He had absented himself from the king's trial, which his wife had twice boldly interrupted, and had even been suspected of planning an eleventh hour rescue of the king.[24] But he still believed in 'Parliament as the King's and the Kingdom's greatest safety.'[25] If these two old friends, the Lord General and Slingsby the 'malignant', could now have met they might have found more agreement than disagreement in their political views.

[1] EHR, 1937, 644. Royalists were deprived of saddles, pistols, corselets, pikes etc., even of fowling pieces, and swords which they normally wore as part of their dress.

[2] F. H. Sunderland, 'Marmaduke, Lord Langdale', 126.
    Arthur, now Lord, Capel was in the siege. He was captured and sent to the Tower whence he escaped, only to be recaptured and tried in Westminster Hall together with the Duke of Hamilton, the Earl of Norwich (Goring), Lord Holland and Owen. The next day he, Hamilton and Holland were executed in Old Palace Yard (D.N.B.).

[3] Diary, 334 – 8.

[4] Sunderland, 145. He was aided in his escape by Philip Dent, the cowman, and vowed that no Dent should ever want while there were Langdales at Houghton. Philip Dent's last descendant was butler to Colonel Philip Langdale in 1914.

[5] Diary, 339.

[6] Arch. Cantiana, II, 186, 187, IX, 38, 42.

[7] Sold to Sir Francis Wythens, Arch. Cantiana, LVIII.

[8] CCC, 867/8. Further trouble was to befall him when in 1655 his younger son murdered the elder son in a fit of jealousy and was publicly hanged. A. Mee, 'Kent', 40.

[9] Evelyn's Diary, II, 560.

[10] CSPD, 1660–1, 16.

[11] Rawl. MS A, 61, p. 35.

12 *Melandre Profugus.*
    Si nullis tenebris laboriosa
    Cessant pectora, pallidaeque curae
    Jam nusquam tepedo annuunt sopori,
    O Di, quis superest locus quieti?

13 EHR, 1937, 643. He, and other delinquents like him, lost all authority in local affairs. The local legend of 'The Bloody Hand' sealing the deer park gates must have originated at this time.

14 Noble, 'Lives of the Regicides'.

15 YAJ, 1930, 409. Alice died 1627 and was buried in Sandal Church.

16 YAJ, 1930, 410.

17 Dr. Barwick, 'Life of Lady Savile', 95 et seq.

18 C. V. Wedgwood, 'The Trial of Charles I', 183.

19 D. Lloyd, 'Memoirs of Lives and Actions'.

20 HMC XIII, Pt. i, 167.

21 YAJ, 1883, 441.

22 J. H. Gray, 'History of the Queens' College', 152. 'Mercurius Aulicus' of 26 August 1643 reported: 'Dr Master Martyn, Master of Queens' College, Cambridge, one of those captive gentlemen that laye under the hatches at Wapping, desiring to gaine above deck as much fresh aire as would keep him alive was by a barbarous villain knocked down upon the floor of the ship and his braines almost beaten out'.

23 HMC Ormonde II.

24 M. A. Gibb, 'The Lord General', 215.

25 M. A. Gibb, 'The Lord General', 34.

Chapter twelve

1650 – 1655

ON THE SURFACE Slingsby's activities were innocent enough – running the estate, making alterations in the garden, teaching his children. His chief recreation was hunting, 'which I can use without exceeding my limitts of five miles, though I can make shift to ride twenty or thirty miles in a daye's hunting – a harmless sport, and not so apt to plott treasons and conspiracies as your Exchang and Westminster Hall.' Apt enough, however, as he well knew, since much of the royalist plotting was done at race meetings and in the hunting field where cavaliers could meet and talk without fear of eavesdroppers. Marston Moor and Salisbury Plain were soon to be named as the most likely rendezvous for royalist risings.

The fact that Redhouse lay beside the river, in an angle between Ouse and Nidd, more than halved the area of Slingsby's five-mile limit. South of the Ouse however there would be good hunting from the ancient 'chace' of the Ughtreds, over Marston Moor or through Thickpenny Farm till checked by the formidable Redhouse Drain (which still holds the record for a jump over water in the hunting field). Redhouse Wood, 120 acres of mixed hardwoods, larch, fir and pine plantations and an almost impenetrable thicket of thorn and elder where the foxes earth, is one of the best coverts in the Ainsty and, in Slingsby's time, might have been even better, both for beast and for royalist plotter. There were foxes then, and the odd buck strayed from the park, though the hare was more often hunted and its habit of

113

running in circles would suit a man who had to keep within limits. The line hounds are taking in Lionel Edwards' sketch of the York and Ainsty leaving Redhouse Wood[1] for Scagglethorpe Moor would have been as familiar to Slingsby as it was to me when I hunted from Redhouse on a black horse with blaze, the double of the one in this picture, descended from Darcy's 'Black-legs Mare.'[2] James Darcy was only a name to me then but he now comes into this story as one of those royalist plotters who, like his elder brother, Colonel Marmaduke, were committed to a royalist rising. Already a supreme council known as the Sealed Knot had been formed, composed of six men who 'had had the most eminent charges in the war . . . and were relations to the greatest families in England.'[3] They were Lord Loughborough, Sir William Compton, Colonels John Russell, Edward Villiers and Sir Richard Willys, and Lord Belasyse, the only Roman Catholic member. The Knot usually met in London and its function was to supervise all royalist plotting in England, to discourage 'absurd and desperate attempts' and to prepare for a general rising when there was a reasonable chance of success.

Its formation had been suggested by Major Nicholas Armorer, a Northumbrian – 'a pretty full and somewhat ruddy-fac't man of middle stature, about 35 or 36 years of age, having a deepe brown hair, short beard and his hair on his head and face much of a colour' – who made many secret journeys between the Court abroad and the northern royalists.[4] Like all other agents, or 'intelligencers,' he had his own cipher, using pseudonyms which began with the first letter of the original. One of Slingsby's was 'Mr. Sanor,' and in the code of another agent, John Cooper, he was 'Mr. Leake' – an odd choice of name for a plotter, especially after his unfortunate dealings with Dr. Leake. Some ciphers were numerical, each number representing a letter. One involved writing the first three letters of a name in numbers, underlined, and the rest as they should be – thus London was written 201,261, 244. DON.[5] Invisible ink – 'powder of gall in water, to be washed over with powder of calcined copper' – was sometimes used;[6] as was lemon juice, on absorbent paper, which became visible only when warmed. One correspondent, writing to his 'Deare Namesake' by this means, pointed out that the last letter the 'deare one' had written was more legible before it was warmed than after, and suggested that he should be more careful over his choice of paper.[7] Most of the royalist ciphers were easily broken, the chief exponent of this being an Oxford don, Dr. John Wallis, Savilian Professor of Geometry, who first deciphered the letters of Charles I after Naseby, and once boasted that he knew of no way of ciphering which he could not discover. Thurloe, 'Cromwell's Master Spy,' had agents everywhere, paying them an average of £10 a month.[8] He also controlled the Post Office, where letters could be intercepted, opened, copied and then sent on. His assistant, Samuel Morland, could forge hand-writing so that not even the writer could detect any difference ; and could copy several sheets of close writing in little more than one minute ; and counterfeit seals and wafers in wax with as sharp an impression as the original.[9] The secret messenger service between London and Yorkshire was said to cost the Yorkshire gentry £25 a week.[10] Since royalist security was poor and Thurloe's spy-ring active it has been rightly said that 'under his eyes in constant review there passed accounts of events, both great and small, which occurred in England or in the capitals and other large cities of Europe.'[11] The news of his sensational leap to safety from the coach which Cromwell was unable to stop, having whipped up the horses to a gallop in Hyde Park, lost nothing in the telling in royalist circles that autumn of 1654.[12]

This was the year that Armorer visited Slingsby at Redhouse to discuss plans for the taking of Hull, the most suitable port for a landing of troops from the Low Countries. Reporting to Hyde from London he wrote 'Mr. Davison of Yorkshire will settle the business of Hull ; he only under-stands it & he is a just and discreet person. Entreat the King to acknowledge the £100 lent to the writer by Sir Henry Slingsby, which is more kindness than he has yet found from any other ; though many have said a great deal more he is our sure friend ; pray therefore forget him not.'[13] The King was 'well satisfied' with the report, and instructed

Hyde to thank Slingsby.[14]

This Mr Davison, the Reverend Charles, an ordained minister and one-time tutor to Sir George Savile[15] at Rufford Abbey, had turned conspirator after being involved in the raid to capture General Rainsborough and exchange him for Langdale, a raid which ended in the accidental killing of Rainsborough. Now, six years later, he had been chosen by the northern royalists to engineer the taking of Hull, and Armorer tells Hyde that all there 'expect great returns from him, for he had a great part of the best stock in his hands.'[16] The next report was less encouraging : 'Davison does not seem to have performed those great services which were expected of him'[17] – any more, Davison implies in subsequent letters, than the lukewarm Sealed Knot had served him. Other agents were also at work in Hull, but with no more success. Charles himself wrote to Colonel Overton, the former parliamentarian Governor now serving in Scotland, promising 'whatever he or his family shall wish' in return for his help.[18] It is doubtful if he ever received the letter. He was already under suspicion for his anti-protectorate views. Continuous efforts were made to win over Fairfax, whom all the moderates would have followed. Charles wrote to Fairfax's brother-in-law, Henry Arthington a prominent presbyterian, in July '54, but without success ; again in September to Sir Philip Monckton at Howden, suggesting further approaches, Monckton himself having several times proposed some sort of kidnapping of Fairfax who lived only 10 miles off ;[19] and finally in October to Lady Fairfax, which letter was delivered to her by Slingsby.[20] But by the end of the year no progress had been made. Fairfax would not be lured from Nun Appleton – his reading and writing, breeding of horses and planning his garden which Andrew Marvell was to immortalise in poetry – by such doubtful prospects and the probable outbreak of a third civil war.

But throughout the year the Action Party in England were busy organising a number of simultaneous risings on a regional basis – in East Anglia, the Midlands, the Welsh Border, the west, London and the home counties, and the north where Slingsby was one of the leaders. It is perhaps significant that in this summer of 1654 he sent his sons, with their servant, abroad.[21] Unluckily for the Action Party its arms-running organisation was discovered on New Years Day, 1655. Many arrests were made and the midland carters, who had been doing well from the delivery of heavy hampers and mysterious crates to various country houses, found themselves short of work. Among those arrested was Colonel Overton, one of the leaders of a Levellers' plot to over-throw the Protector and set up a commonwealth. The Levellers' rendezvous, Salisbury Plain and Marston Moor, and the date fixed for their rising, were the same as those of the royalists – 6 February.[22]

But the whole royalist design was weakened by rivalries between the Action Party who wanted immediate action, and the Sealed Knot who preached caution, rivalries which it was virtually impossible for Charles in absence to heal. The date of the risings was first postponed from 6 to 13 February, and then again to 9 March. Charles sent a message to the Knot: 'Nor can it be reasonable for me to hinder them [the Action Party] from movinge who believe themselves ready for it, and undone if they do not, and yett I cannot looke for any greate success if, whilst they stirr, you sitt still.'[23] This equivocal message was carried by Daniel O'Neill and Armorer, who had the misfortune to be detained under suspicion at Dover Castle where all passengers were scanned by soldiers lining the walled walk that led up to the Castle and then had their papers examined in the Custom House. Armorer, posing as Nicholas Wright, with urgent family business to attend to in Newcastle, talked his way out. But O'Neill, the bearer of the letter, was held for another eight precious days. 'I am very much troubled at Wright's being released,' wrote Thomas Wilson, the Deputy Governor, from Dover Castle in reply to an angry letter from Thurloe, who had circulated instructions for a strict examination of all passengers from Holland, 'especially considering that particular bloudy design you mention . . . I wish with all my heart I had been there, but I trust the Lord will graciously disappoint his horrid intentions.'[24] In the meantime Rochester, the reckless cheerful companion of Charles's wanderings after Worcester and now appointed

Field Marshal General 'to command next and immediately under Us and Our said most dear Brother,' had crossed via Margate and reached London on the same day as did O'Neill, 24 February, only twelve days before the day appointed for the risings. Five of those days he spent in London secretly meeting the regional agents in the shop of an Aldgate Street tailor who described him as a fat, round-faced, clean-shaven man in a yellow periwig,[25] meetings he told Charles, with unfounded optimism, which 'had brought all the creditors to such a composition as we hope will not disappoint you.'[26] But a warning note had come from the west where a number of Somerset conspirators, who had not been notified of the change of date, had rendezvoused in Salisbury and been arrested, among them Walter Slingsby, released only recently from the Tower. Nevertheless, as the agents left for their respective regions, Rochester and Armorer set off for Yorkshire, relying on false information that Fairfax would emerge and so make this the decisive area where the Field Marshal General should be. But the man the Yorkshiremen had all along asked for, Marmaduke Langdale, was not permitted by the Court to come, probably because it was thought his catholicism might prejudice such potential allies as the presbyterian Fairfax. Much preparatory work had been done by Armorer, Davison, Darcy, Robert Walters and Sir Richard Mauleverer (son of the regicide). Darcy had brought £1000 from the meagre royalist funds abroad; Mauleverer had 'ridden from family to family, they met under the pretence of hunting and the like';[27] Robert Walters, who had been Mauleverer's Lt. Colonel of Horse at the siege of Colchester, a pale, thin-faced, brown-haired veteran[28] and indefatigable in his journeys to and from the continent, had obtained promises from more than 1500 royalists to meet Rochester on Marston Moor. With him was his brother, John, an officer in Bristol's regiment sent from France ostensibly to buy horses for his commanding officer and bring them back.[29]

In less than a week Rochester reached Cattal Hall, the home of Sir William Ingram, old Arthur's nephew and one of Charles I's Colonels of Foot, which was to be their headquarters for the next three days. The Hall, on the site of the present Old Thorneville Hall, lay beside the Nidd which winds between high banks round the north-west edge of Marston Moor and is crossed hereabouts by only two bridges, Cattal Bridge and Skip Bridge. In that space of three days Rochester had to work hard. He did not know the terrain, not having fought in the north. He did not know how many of the 1500 would turn out. He probably did not know the strength of the fifth columnists in York, which was his main objective. All he did know was that a nearly full moon would rise at 10 o'clock on the night of the 8th and that 'The Bloody Almanack' for 1655, in its long-range weather forecast based on the movements of the celestial bodies, had prudently said that March would have 'cold mornings and somewhat windy on the 1st, 6th and 7th dayes, and some sharp and sudden showrs towards the latter end.'[30] For the rest he had to rely on the men on the spot – Slingsby, Darcy, Ingram, Mauleverer – all with fine records of service. But it is clear, from the report that 'he solicited people very strongly and threatened some,'[31] that he was a worried man. A Yorkshire leader like Langdale would not have had to do this for, as Slingsby had said, he so won the hearts of his men that 'they cared not which way they went so long as they followed him.'

Rochester 'fully stinted [timed himself] to have been in York that night' writes Thomas Burton, and York was said to be ready to receive him. But first he had to assemble his force at some rendezvous easily found by night – a corner of Wilstrop Wood, or Four Lanes Meet whence the eastern track led to an ancient paved way from Hessay to York which fugitives from the battle had followed, also by night.[32] Surprise was essential, perhaps by 'carters' going in in the early hours, overpowering the guards and seizing one of the gates, backed up by fifth columnists in the city. The horse could then spur in and scour the streets shouting victorious slogans, followed by the foot whose march had been speeded up by having their body armour carried in the carts. 1500 men was a minimum force for such an operation. As it was only a paper one, the whole business was desperately chancy.

1 Lionel Edwards, 'My Hunting Sketch Book' Vol i, 24.
2 C. M. Prior, 'The Royal Studs of the 16th and 17th Centuries', 98, By Deed of Appointment James Darcy was made Master of the Royal Studs in June 1660, his predecessor having been Sir John Fenwick.
3 Clarendon Con. 63.
4 TSP IV, 164.
5 Cl. MSS. 12.
6 CClSP II, 391.
7 TSP VI, 869.
8 Hobman, 'Cromwell's Master Spy', 22.
9 HMC Buccleuch II, 48–51.
10 Underdown, 139.
11 Hobman, 14.
12 Nicholas Papers II. 108.
13 CClSP II, 336.
14 CClSP II, 347.
15 Son of Sir William Savile and later created first marquis of Halifax. The Saviles moved to Rufford Abbey after Thornhill was burnt.
16 CClSP II, 335.
17 CClSP II, 377.
18 CClSP II, 344.
19 Monckton Papers, 42–43.
20 CClSP III, 59.
21 CSPD 1654, 440.
22 EHR 1888–9, 329.
23 CClSP III, 16. Clar MSS. xlix, fol, 340.
24 TSP III, 164.
25 EHR 1888–9, 314.
26 Eva Scott, 'Travels of the King', 76.
27 T. Burton, i, 230–1.
28 Royalist Composition Papers, 26 January 1652.
29 Rawl. MS A, 9, 171.
30 British Museum, E 816, 1.
31 T. Burton, 230–1.
32 Surtees Society 1875, Yorks Diaries, 139.

Chapter Thirteen

1655 – 1656

WHAT ACTUALLY HAPPENED on the night of the 8th must be pieced together from odd scraps of information. Mauleverer assembled his tenants at his home at Allerton Mauleverer and gave them a great supper before setting off for the rendezvous.[1] Others probably did the same – his near neighbour Richard Hutton in the tall gabled hall beside Goldsborough church, and Robert Walters at Little Ouseburn. From further north came Colonel Sir Jordan Crosland of Newby Hall overlooking the Ure, Robert Brandling from Leathley and Walter Strickland from Thornton Bridge by the fast-flowing Swale. Marmaduke Darcy from Sedbury had the furthest distance to cover and Slingsby the shortest. Nidd, Swale, Ure and Ouse were each represented by this trickle of royalists with their followers, but the full flood, which might have swept through York and then on to Hull, never reached Marston Moor. The numbers that did were a bare tenth of those expected. Others were said to have been waiting, all saddled up and ready to move when they heard how many had assembled. Rochester failed in the darkness to get control even over these few. *Mercurius Politicus*, one of the parliamentary newsletters of the time, thus reported the affair :[2] 'Friday last sennight about midnight about 200 Papists and Cavaliers met at Hessam Moor (alias Marston Moor, a place where 25,000 of them were heretofore soundly beaten) who brought with them to the said moor 5–600 arms, muskets, pikes etc., where they expected a great appearance by a general rise of that gang and designed to have seized York that night, which feasibly might have been done. Amongst them were sundry Frenchmen who are fled; some of the meaner sort, being discovered and apprehended, have discovered many; amongst the rest are Sir William Ingram, a man of little action, who yet secured many of them in his house 3 or 4 days before this appearance. He, being but a timerous man, by the genius of Colonel Lilburne hath confest and laid all naked; and it is verily believed the Scots King was at his house, by all description . . . The Colonel hath secured many Gentlemen, some that will be found faulty, others upon suspicion.' According to another report the panic was caused by 'three men travelling over the moor who chanced to lose their way, one holloing one unto another and keeping up a great noise, which struck the others with fear so that they dispersed, everyone shifting for himself, leaving many arms which were since found thrown in the whins and all up and down the moor.'[3] One eye-witness saw four cartloads of arms brought into York the next day. 'The Lord doth scatter and confound this phrentick generation in their conspiracies,' continues the reporter, 'the like we are to expect to hear of them from other parts, knowing they imbarque in a cause that will sink all its owners and defenders. How much then doth it concern all sober men to be active in resolution for the maintenance of the publick Peace.' Thurloe sententiously summed up the affair 'It's true it fell not out according to their intention. The great reason of all was, the Lord disappointed them and gave us occasion to say of them "They conceived mischief, they travelled in iniquity etc!" Other subordinate causes were, It pleased God to discover a great part of their plott.'[4]

The cavaliers had different reasons. The absence of Langdale and Fairfax's neutrality have already been mentioned. In addition Lord Belasyse, the Yorkshire representative in the Sealed Knot, stayed at home in London avoiding involvement. Walter Strickland was particularly blamed for precipitately fleeing and causing Marmaduke Darcy, whom he met coming late with 60 men, also to turn, word of which must have reached others who were also wondering whether to come or not to this very local assembly of neighbours, most of whom lived within a radius of 5 or 6 miles of the moor. Those who had come were blamed for not waiting longer; but for many the moor held memories which certainly would not dissolve in those lonely hours of darkness there. 'Strangely frightened with their own shaddows,' Colonel Lilburne wrote, 'they fled to their own homes where they thought they should have rested undiscovered.'[5] But the main cause of the failure was the confusion over dates. Communication was necessarily slow (as had been shown in the Salisbury fiasco) and some must have wondered whether the 8th March would not also be changed, perhaps to the ominous Ides, a week later. Rochester, shaken by his experience, refused to fix a later date and after an angry scene, in which he blamed the northerners for deceiving him and they blamed royalist headquarters for mis-management and forbidding Langdale to come, he and Armorer took the road south.

The hunt was up. 'If he [Rochester] had not been a man very fortunate in disguises,' wrote Clarendon, 'he would certainly never have escaped so many perambulations; for as he was the least wary in making his journeys in safe hours, so he departed very unwillingly from all places where there was good eating and drinking, and entered into conferences with any strangers he met or joined with.'[6] They would have been caught at an inn in Aylesbury if the innkeeper had not too literally followed the local constable's instructions to keep an eye on the two strange horses in his stables instead of on their riders. 'Rochester's escape at Aylesbury cost him deare on being compelled to part with his gold chain,' wrote Captain Peter Mews to Secretary Nicholas; 'better that than his head.' The writer then went on to describe how Rochester had disguised himself as a grazier with 'brave basket hilt sword tyed up to his back . . . but bee very silent in this particular for it might be much to Rochester's prejudice if some heere should know it and hee yet in England.'[7] So much for royalist security! In spite of this he and Armorer escaped and joined the court which had moved to Bruges where Charles was living in a house behind the Belfry, now a Flemish beer-cellar. Armorer, forced by a shortage of accommodation, had to stay in an expensive inn (where the royal horses were stabled) to his great annoyance.[8] In Bruges, under the external frivolities of this 'Venice of the North,' plans for another rising were being ardently discussed.

Mauleverer rode home, said good-bye to his wife, and made for Cheshire where he and John Walters were captured and imprisoned in Chester. Not for long for 'under colour of his devotions, to which he had accustomed himself often every day, and by the help of a woman (said to have been his wife) who is gone and not yet heard of, and by the help of her apparel . . . he escaped forth at a window down into the street, and after him went Mr. Walters,' as Captain John Griffiths reported to Thurloe, 'and no sign of them in spite of search parties, hu-an-cryes and posts to all partes, and myself been forth all night and all day,' No wonder he signed himself 'Your very affectionate although weary and perplexed servant.'[9]

Robert Walters took the road south. He was caught somewhere but escaped, after which, in a wood near Barkway (the Hertfordshire village where his cousin, Robert Slingsby, was living) he tore up the list he was carrying of all those 'gentlemen and others' who had promised to turn out on Marston Moor.[10] He ultimately reached Gravesend but, while looking for a boat to Rotterdam, was seized by five of Thurloe's agents – who sent in a bill for £2. 10s. to cover their expenses – and taken to the Marshalsea Gaol for cross-examination.[11] 'I verily believe,' wrote one of his captors, 'that upon assurance of life he would divulge whatsoever concerned that business, and who were engaged in itt, which perchance may bee of more consequence than his life.'[12] But Lilburne, writing to Thurloe from York, predicted more truly 'I much doubt you will not get much out of Walters by reason we have proceeded against his wife here,'[13] she and her children having been evicted from their Little Ouseburn estate which a certain Alderman Dickinson had long coveted, since it lay adjacent to his own.[14]

Lilburne was hot on the trail of all who had been at the Marston Moor gathering and, appealing against an order

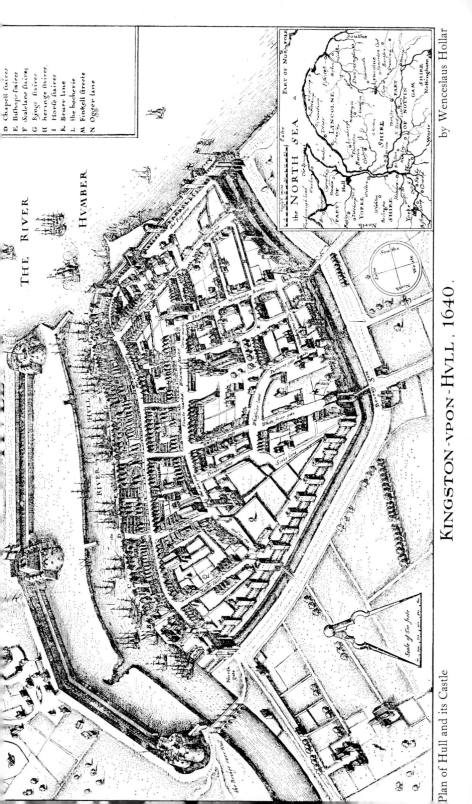

D Chapell staires
E Bishops staires
F Scalelane staires
G Kings staires
H heringe staires
I Horse staires
K Brure lane
L the bocherie
M Finkell streete
N Ogger lane

THE RIVER

HVMBER

THE RIVER

HVLL

Plan of Hull and its Castle

KINGSTON-VPON-HVLL, 1640.

by Wenceslaus Hollar

The fine linen shirt in which Sir Henry Slingsby was executed on Tower Hill, 8 June 1658. *(By permission of the Borough of Harrogate Public Library.*

from Lambert to send some of his regiment to Lancashire, wrote 'If I spare any more troops many considerable persons that were at the rendezvous will be untaken where they thought they should have rested undisturbed.'[15]

Slingsby was one of them, betrayed, according to local tradition, by his Beningbrough neighbour, Sir John Bourchier, the regicide, who watched his movements from the other side of the river, and reported that he had seen him walking on the leads of Redhouse. Bourchier had been hostile to royalists ever since he had suffered imprisonment and a heavy fine for objecting to Charles I's hunting in what he considered his own park in the Forest of Galtres when the king was staying in York in 1633 as Sir Arthur Ingram's guest.[16] His enemies said of him that he had 'God in his mouth and the Devil in his heart.' Whether or not he was the betrayer, Slingsby was seized one evening, as he walked down to the deer park, by a doorway in the peach wall, now bricked up, where his would-be captors could wait under cover in the orchard on the other side of the wall, and then corner him. They took him under strong guard to Hull. The next official information comes in a letter from Lilburne to Thurloe, written on 25 January, 1656 :[17] 'We are now upon the business of the late plotters. We had Sir Henry Slingsby before us today and was readie to pass sentence upon him, but that he desired time to make some defence tomorrow, which in justice we could not denie . . . We got soe much from the mouth of Colonel Brandling today as (I think) will serve his turne without any further proofe.' In his next letter of 14 March to Cromwell Lilburne writes :[18] 'We do here inclosed send you a list of such persons, with qualifications and additions, as have been convened before us and found guilty . . . whereupon we have secured their persons, viz. Sir Henry Slingsby, Col. Brandling, Henry Darcy, Walter Strickland, Sutton Oglethorpe, William Frankland and Captain John Croft and Richard Hutton Esq. being men of quality, in the garrison of Hull . . . the rest of them being men of mean quality are secured in the common gaol for the County of York, and such of them as have estates are sequestered.' Alderman Dickinson may have smiled as he added his name to those of the other five signatories. For another estate was going for some other opportunist, Lilburne having reported that though Lady Mauleverer had pleaded innocence 'she appears to be of a very dangerous spirit and to have bin active in the late plot, and a promoter of it' and that therefore 'it would be of evil consequence' to restore her to her home.[19] He was quickly finding the answer to the question he had once asked Thurloe 'What do you do in general with such kind of cattle?'

Meanwhile the 'cattle' had to await trial by jury.[20] A Commission was appointed to meet in York on 20 April, but was not ready by that date. Lilburne, anxious over the result of such a trial, asked Thurloe if he had consulted the judges 'in this weighty case, wherein if there should be any lameness, or so much knottiness that the naile cannot be driven into the head, it were better not to enter upon it in this way . . . As for jurors, happily the law may give liberty to choose them without the liberties of this city, then we shall do pretty well.'[21] For, of course, the chosen jurors had to be 'honest and well affected to His Highness and the present government.' The Solicitor General himself also had his doubts and wrote to Thurloe from Grantham on his way north to ask whether he should go on to York, since 'the evidence doesn't seem so clear and plain as I did apprehend it would have been.' Unless witnesses were assured that they would not be proceeded against their evidence would be worthless. 'The testimony in this case ought to be very clear and evident of the plott, designe and intention of these men ; a jury will hardly be perswaded that meeting together, though in such a manner as they did, and going away without effecting more, is high treason.'[22] The three judges themselves had their doubts over the constitutionalism of Cromwell's treason ordinance, and so were dismissed and others less scrupulous were appointed. Even they found the prisoners guilty only of riot and released them on bail.[23] But not Slingsby and the 'seven other persons of quality' who were sentenced to indefinite imprisonment in Hull, without the intervention of a jury, because it was impossible to obtain a verdict in these northern parts.'

1   Underdown, 'Royalist Conspiracy in England', 140.
2   Mercurius Politicus 1654–5. 5210.
3   Mercurius Politicus 1654–5. 5209.
4   TSP IV 132.
5   TSP III 226.
6   Clarendon XIV, 135–6.
7   Nicholas Papers II, 327.
8   Eva Scott, 'Travels of the King'.
9   Clarke Papers III, 31.
10 TSP III, 722.
11 SPDI 102, fol. 231.
12 TSP III, 722.
13 TSP IV 498
14 HMC 7th Report App. 97a.
15 TSP III 226.
16 HMC Cowper II, 33. There is a reference here to a letter delivered to Mistress Fulwood, then at Redhouse, about 'Sir John Bourchier and the rest of the actors in that insolent and contemptuous riot' who were awaiting trial in prison.
17 TSP IV 462.
18 TSP IV 614.
19 YAJ 1879, 94–5.
20 Drake in his 'Eboracum' writes, p. 288, that a walk by the Fosse in York Castle was called 'Sir Harry's Walk, said to be made by that unfortunate gentleman in his confinement in this Castle'. This must have been while awaiting trial by jury.
21 TSP III 359–60.
22 TSP III 373.
23 CCISP III 59.

Chapter Fourteen

1657

THE OTHER REGIONAL RISINGS planned for this date proved as fruitless as the Yorkshire one and wholesale arrests followed the establishment of government by Major-Generals. Lambert was Major-General for the north, with Lilburne as his deputy for Yorkshire.[1] The only rising where shots were fired was Penruddock's in the west, and this in spite of the confusion over dates which had caused the arrest of Walter Slingsby who would once more have need of the prayers he had composed during his earlier imprisonment in the Tower, and written out in a fair hand in a little book, entitled 'A Mission of Consolation, usefull for all afflicted Persons,'[2] especially that prayer made on the day of the solar eclipse of 2 August, 1654 – 'Do, Lord, as thou art now about mercifully to remove this darkness and to restore the perfect light of the sun to the world, so be graciously pleased to destroy sin and darkness in our souls, that we may sitt eternally in the light of thy glorious presence.'

One ray of more terrestrial light reached Slingsby in prison in a letter brought by John Cooper, dated 16 April 1656, from Charles, and handed to him by John Walters,[3] which read : 'If I have said nothing to you of the sense I have of your troubles, since you fell into them, it was for fear of encreasing them ; but now that I have met with a secure way of writing to you I cannot forbear to let you know that I shall never forget the care of your sufferings and that I hope it will not be long before you will be freed from them. The

128

particular reason of my hopes and present desires to you I will refer to the person by whose conveyance you will receive this, remaining Yours . . .' What neither Charles nor Slingsby knew was that by now Walters was in Thurloe's pay and had handed in this letter for a copy to be made in Thurloe's office before delivering it.[4] So much for the King's 'secure way of writing !'

John Cooper, as loyal as Walters was false, had been at the centre of the Rufford Abbey rising with Davison. He had been captured but escaped by throwing pepper in the guard's eyes, and got overseas, to become a regular courier between Langdale and the royalists in England. He used numbers and pseudonyms, his own signature reading 9.39.40.41.14.49.[5] Now he impatiently awaited a reply, via Walters, from Slingsby and at last, on May Day was able to write to Armorer : 'Mr. Thompson [Walters] is returned from Leake [Slingsby] and goes tomorrow to Mr. Allen [Rochester]. Mr. Leake is willing to accommodate Mr. Conyers [the King] but the proportion I know not, nor the way, for 'tis by his sonn whoe is in your parts.'[6] Armorer was then in Bruges and Slingsby's sons, who had gone abroad two years earlier, were probably there too. So was Charles, living in considerable poverty and grateful for any financial help such as was here promised.

The offer of another sort of accommodation came a fortnight later from Arthur Slingsby, who put his house in the park at Brussels at the king's disposal if he should come to meet Don Juan, the new Viceroy of the Spanish Nether-lands.[7] This house was soon to figure in a scandalous episode. As part of an alleged plot to disprove Lucy Walters' marriage to Charles and get her son, the future Duke of Monmouth, away from her, she was persuaded to lodge in Arthur's house where he was to effect the separation 'in as quiet a way as he could.'[8] His efforts ended in a street brawl in which the mother clung screaming to her son. Arthur was reprimanded. But on telling Charles that she had compromising papers in her trunk he was ordered to search it. Whereupon she threatened to post up all the king's letters to her unless her pension was paid.[9] Finally she agreed to let the boy 'be bred up and instructed as the King approved' provided she could live in Brussels in any house but Arthur's.[10] Soon after this he received a baronetcy and the next year she died.

A more pressing problem for Charles to face was how to secure a port for landing the army of invasion. John Walters, who had returned to the continent after visiting Slingsby, reported to Thurloe that he had seen Rochester and that there was 'other business in hand. They are mightily in hopes and have still designes on some towns. I know not how you can write to me safely ; my name hereafter will be John Halle.'[11] Hull was still the most suitable port. It contained the largest magazine in the country, with equipment for 16,000 men and, once taken, could easily be held. The Castle, which comprised three blockhouses joined by a wall ¾ mile in length, had been built by order of Henry VIII when, with his fifth Queen, Catherine Howard (beheaded only six months later) he visited the city and 'was magnificently and splendidly entertained for three days.'[12] Much of the building material, including some gravestones, came from religious houses he had suppressed – the Blackfriary, Whitefriary and Carthusian Priory of Swine. The blockhouses were built in the shape of a club on a playing card, with an entrance in the stem, or base, dungeons on the three arms and a courtyard in the centre.[13] The Castle guarded the mouth of the River Hull and its 16 foot walls were so strongly constructed that blasting was needed to demolish them 300 years later. If Cromwell had believed all that the Mayor and Burgesses told him in their loyal address of December 1653, in which they thanked God for keeping them from 'being consumed in the middle of the burning bush . . . and for using His Highness, as He had used Moses, to bring his people out of Egypt and Babylon, to be a glorious intrument in promising for us a safe, happy and settled peace by sea,' he could have rested content.[14] Hull had certainly remained quiet in the '55 rising, possibly because the two most ardent East Riding royalists, Langdale and Monckton, had not been involved, and because Overton the Leveller, was by then in the Tower.

Nevertheless 'An accompt of the garrison at Hull,' prepared by Colonel Bury and sent to Cromwell in March of 1655, must have caused him considerable concern.[15] Though the garrison was said to be efficient, the magazine could not be kept dry, the fortifications were much 'out of repair and the guns and carriages of all gt peices rott and destroyed.' The Colonel recommended that the garrison of 500 should be doubled by trained men, not recruits, for 'a place of so great concernment is nott to be kept with men either unexperienced or unknown,' and that a bar should be built across the mouth of the harbour to prevent fire ships or landing craft slipping in under cover of darkness. For further security he advised the removal of John Canne, the garrison chaplain whom Overton had appointed, for 'he doth disservice amongst the soldiery, his spirits not agreeing with the government.' Canne had found a rival in Master John Shaw, an ex-army chaplain and indefatigable preacher, who had been minister of the Low Church and Trinity Church since 1644. At the end of the war he had accompanied Pembroke and Northumberland when they went to Newcastle to treat with the Scots and, of course, preached there. Shaw resented the intervention of this newcomer who 'broached many fond opinions and drew away the Governor and his wife and some others,' as he wrote in his Diary.[16] Overton, the then Governor, had even had a thick wall built across Trinity Church so that Canne, the Independent, could preach to him and the garrison in the chancel while Shaw, the presbyterian – 'a Boanerges wielding divine thunder' – preached to a congregation which he estimated at over three thousand.

The connection of this ministerial rivalry with our story is that round about 1658 an anonymous letter, possibly written by Shaw (who also preached on occasion at Hampton Court and Whitehall and so had some influence) was sent to Cromwell.[17] Its object was to draw his attention to the weaknesses of the garrison and defences of Hull. The writer urges that ' a strict discipline be kept over the army, that Bacchus may keep his Revells noe longer where Man should keep his Schools – the Lord knows how sinn abounds by drinking, whoring and swearing'. Twelve years, he says, is too long for the same three companies to have remained on garrison duty. As for their officers, they 'minde nothing but Hawking and hunting, seldom looking to their charges, which might give a fair opportunity to Cavaleeres or others to attempt a surprise raide.' Only half the companies were present except at muster and they 'are given such liberty and are so negligent that I durst venture my life I could surprise either of the blockhouses or the Castle with 30 men.' Fifty men in each blockhouse and the Castle, 'with beds to lodge in constantly there, under honest and trusty Officers, woulde keepe them more securely than they were kept yett,' for most of the men slept out with their wives in town or country. Though wishing there was still 'recipocall affection between Your Highness and Colonel Overton that there was once,' to restore which he 'would tread 500 miles afoot,' he admits that the present Governor, Colonel Henry Smith, is 'a solid sober-spiritted Gentleman.' After exhorting the Protector to strengthen the bonds of unity between all Protestant Princes and States against the anti-Christian powers of Rome the writer ends on an ever-familiar theme – the price of beer, which had risen so much since the new tax on malt 'that I never heard the like outcrye in all my life ; if it continue Travellers will be troubled to get accommodation on the roads, neither will there be any Beare to be had for the men of warr in this part' – or for thirsty preachers ![18]

This was how Master John Shaw (or whoever the writer was) saw those who guarded Hull and its prisoners, and doubtless the royalist agents were equally aware of the situation. Whether Cromwell ever read the letter is another matter. He had much else to worry him. Since the abortive royalist and Levellers' risings of '55 royalism had been driven underground by the arrests or close surveillance of suspected leaders under the régime of the Major Generals. The only immediate hope of the more desperate lay in Cromwell's death by assassination and many warnings of plots, both royalist and Leveller, reached his ears. 'Richard Rose, Lord Wilmot's servant,' wrote an agent to Thurloe, 'who hath a wart on his left eyelid, is just now sent to England with letters or a message to put on the murdering of the Protector.'[19] Reports were received of a series of lethal weapons – 'a stone-bow, blunderbusses concealed in viol cases, an engine that would doe execution upon the tyrant's person at least 300 yards distance,' a fire bomb placed in the chapel of Whitehall – or of ambush as he rode to Hampton Court by shooting, from a house in Hammersmith, with guns that carried twelve bullets. A 'most excellent treatise entitled "Killing no Murder"' was in circulation, 'shewing both scriptural and many reasons that it is not only lawfull but even necessary to kill him, being a usurper and tyrant who ought noe more to have any law than a wolf or a fox.'[21] Charles Davison had been involved in one plot in the autumn of '55 which failed. And Armorer, soon after his escape from Yorkshire, had sent his servant Thomas Pearce to make another attempt[22] – 'the new one gone with this passage' as reported to Thurloe, with the further information that 'there isn't a passage but eyther brings or carryes over some of their creatures. This last week came over a gentleman of the Lord Wilmot's, who brought over horses and hounds for Charles Stuart.' Pearce was arrested in January '56, though in the meantime he had received a letter from his master conveying greetings to Mr Sanor (Slingsby),[23] who would certainly have condemned these plots, as did other responsible royalists, notably Monckton. Many of them also mistrusted the secret Treaty of Brussels which had been discussed, if not signed, in Arthur Slingsby's house there.[24] Under the terms Spain, in return for the restoration of Jamaica and suspension of the penal laws against the catholics in England, was to provide an invading army of 6000 from the Spanish Netherlands as soon as an English port was secured. This made command of the sea and the guarding of Hull more vital than ever for the government. For, though Spain had demanded a rising in England to be followed by invasion, she was being urged to reverse the order and a fleet of Dutch transports was already assembled to embark the troops. The Hull design was still on the agenda of Royalist conspiracy. Langdale was reported to have been seen talking to 'two ancient gentlemen' at Flushing who were about to be taken to Hull. Much was expected of a Captain Thomas Gardiner, who incidentally was Overton's brother-in-law. But he was rash enough in August '57 to visit a kinswoman employed in the household of Richard Cromwell at Hampton

Court, where his curiosity about the Protector's movements and whether or not he wore a bullet-proof vest, and the finding on him of two loaded pistols (which he said he carried lest he met his Major, who bore him a grudge) led to his immediate arrest, and the end of his activities in Hull.[25]

Throughout this year, 1657, preparations for regional risings were once more being vigorously prosecuted, but far less thoroughly than for the '55 risings, mainly due to lack of competent leaders. In the south John Mordaunt and Dr. Hewitt, whose destinies were to be linked with Slingsby's, were busy organising the Surrey and Sussex royalists. Mordaunt was the younger son of the first Earl of Peterborough and had been imprisoned for raising a regiment of horse in the '48 rising in Surrey. Since then he had been working for a broad alliance of parliamentary and presbyterian leaders with the royalists, helped by the fact that his father had served under Essex as a parliamentary commander and his mother was a strong puritan. Dr. Hewitt had been chaplain to the Lifeguard of Foot in the war and was now one of the most popular preachers in London at the little church of St. Gregory by St. Paul's, patronised by royalists – and by Evelyn who constantly commends his sermons. One member of his congregation was Mary, Cromwell's third daughter, soon to be married, to everyone's astonishment, to Lord Fauconberg, Slingsby's nephew. Cromwell had taken considerable trouble to find out all he could about this influential young widower and had asked Lockhart, the English ambassador in Paris where Fauconberg then was, for a confidential report on his character and financial security.[26] With this he was fully satisfied, Mary received a dowry of £15,000 and Hewitt married them according to the rites of the Church of England after the official public ceremony. At first they lived with Cromwell in their own suite of rooms, sometimes at Hampton Court, sometimes at Whitehall.[27] But they must have been as well aware of the dangers that threatened him from all sides as he himself was.

The various plots being hatched were well known to the authorities and by January 1658 the Governors of strategic places had been alerted. But Ormond, at the request of the

Spaniards, in order to get first-hand information, crossed in disguise with O'Neill and landed at Westmarsh, near Colchester, where they spent that night, too cold to go to bed, in an inn, playing shuffle-board and drinking mulled ale with four maltsters.[28] Reaching London he met most of the leaders of the planned risings and evaded capture, in spite of having dyed his hair with a mixture which turned it all colours, by moving from lodging to lodging. The pursuit at last got too hot, but not before he had formed the opinion that, though there was little cohesion between the regional plots and too much was left to chance, it only required a landing by Charles on English soil for all Cromwell's enemies to join the invading force. If Hull could not be secured, the best alternative was Yarmouth, where the Spaniards would be able to land before Cromwell could collect enough forces there to prevent them. But valuable time had been lost while Ormond was in England and the renewed blockade of Ostend made it impossible for the troopships to put to sea. The English coasts were patrolled by frigates, and cavaliers and catholics were once more confined within the five-mile limit. More arrests were made, including those of two Yorkshiremen, Sir Jordan Crosland and Sir Philip Monckton, who were imprisoned in Hull; and of Mordaunt and Hewitt in the south, betrayed by one of the Sussex leaders, John Stapley, whom they had trusted.

1   Firth & Davies, 258.
2   Add MS 38647.
3   CClSP III, 112.
4   Rawl MS 37. 182. The copy is endorsed in Thurloe's hand: 'Charles Stuart's letter of 16th April to Sir Henry Slingsby, brought by John Cooper and delivered to John Walters to be conveyed to Slingsby. It was delivered to me by Walters on 16th April (Old Style); having taken a copy thereof I gave it to Walters to be conveyed as he had direction'.
5   Underdown, 348.
6   CClSP III, 129.
7   CClSP III, 131. Eva Scott 'Travels of the King', 214.

8   CCISP III 394.
9   CCISP III 400–1.
10 CCISP III 396.
11 CSPD 1655–6. 319
12 Tickell, 'History of Hull', 852.
13 Sheahan. 'History of Hull', 265.
14 Tickell, 499.
15 TSP III, 239.
16 Surtees Society, 'Life of John Shaw'. 1875, 134.
17 Add. MS 4159, fol. 105.
18 TSP IV 468. Robert Lilburne, writing to Cromwell on 26 January 1655, enclosed a letter recommending the tax on 'ale and beere which will be an addition to the yearly profitt it affords Your Highness and take away those grave abuses in the present collection thereof' by excisemen, many of whom were 'desperate Cavaliers'.
19 CSPD 1655, 213
20 Clarke Papers III, 40.
21 Eva Scott 324.
22 TSP IV, 206.
23 Rawl MS A 33. 748–57.
24 CCISP IV, 105.
25 TSP VI, 447.
26 TSP VI, 134.
27 R. W. Ramsey, 'Studies in Cromwell's Family Circle',
28 Carte, 'Life of Ormond', Vol III, 660, 665. Eva Scott, 328.

Chapter Fifteen

1657 – 1658

THOUGH THE CHANCES of securing Hull for the landing of an invading force seemed remote Slingsby had not been idle. For nearly two years he had been living on parole and without a guard in a house in the town and Henry, his younger son, appears to have lived, or at least stayed, with him from time to time, and to have fraternised with some of the garrison officers, especially a Lieutenant Thompson. Towards the end of '57 however the Governor, Colonel Henry Smith, told Thurloe that he was becoming suspicious of Slingsby's activities. As a result he was sent certain orders, not extant, for on 4 February he wrote to Cromwell :[1] 'According to Your Highness's commands of 30th January I have endeavoured all the wayes and means that possibly I could to get further proofs against Sir Henry Slingsby, besides Major Waterhouse, but I cannot by any means accomplish it for the present. I have desired the Major to use all the arguments that hee could to persuade him to engage a friend of his in the plott who should be a messenger betwixt them, for the better carrying on of the busyness. But he would not condescend to it, telling the Major it would be dangerous to both of them to have any other made privy to it till nearer the time of putting things into execution. I have sent herewith inclosed in the Major's letter the severall overtures by him to Sir Henry Slingsby and the passages betwixt them ; whereby Your Highness may understand how far they have proceeded. I am doubtfull that Major Waterhouse will be very much troubled when I shall furnish the South Blockhouse with other soldiers, but I will endeavour to preserve a right understanding betwixt us'. That the Major was indeed troubled is evident from the letter he wrote to the Protector, in a scrawl that contrasts with the Colonel's copy-book writing :[2] 'To afford me pardon in this my address, which may justly be called insolency, or at least by your more favourable construction, presumption, I present Your Highness in all humility with the inclosed overtures made by Sir Henry Slingsby again to envelop these nations under your most happy government in bloody warre, and that by a peice of treacherie so deplorable that my heart trembles to think and toung falters to express it.' He trusts however that he will be able to uncover the plot 'by the blessing of God who is not only able to make the feeble strong, the fearfull valiant, but also to fitt and qualify men of a low and mean capacity to serve you who Hee in mercy hath set above me. I know the hazard I have run in this undertaking, not being commissionated thereto by your sacred self; yet conscience tells me that I am bound both in honour and honesty, though with the loss of my liff which I have now laid at your feet, to serve you with faythfulness and with all humility and duty subscribes himself Your Highness most faythfull and humble servant, Ra. Waterhouse'.

One thing he was apparently not allowed to try was to get a commission out of Slingsby, for the Governor complained to Thurloe that 'if His Highness had given way to it, the Major would have had a commission very shortly from Charles Stuart . . . which would have been good evidence against him and have convicted others'.[3] But by now the Governor, beginning to fear that Slingsby might 'have some notice of the busyness' and try to escape, told Cromwell he had secured him in the Castle, 'where he had not been many dayes but that he manifested his malicious treacherie against Your Highness and endeavoured to engage Captain Overton in the same treacherous design . . . but hath not yett proceeded so far as he did with Major Waterhouse. When the busyness is ripe I shall dispose of him according to Your Highness commands'.[4] That Slingsby had had 'some notice' and taken measures to safeguard himself in case he was sent before a jury (some of whom could always be bribed or otherwise influenced) seems evident from a letter, vaguely worded so as not to compromise himself, which he wrote to his son at York. 'Harry,' it reads, 'concerning two men who are of the jury, I would not have you fail to speak with your friend about them, that they may not fail to be at the assizes ; and if it be possible let him speak with the rest of the twelve, for it concerns your friend's business very much. You had need of an expositor ; therefore let the lawyer see this letter and commend me to him, Your loving Father, Hen. Slingsbie, 22 March. P.S. When he hath seen it, burn this letter. Major Waterhouse is pleased to deliver it to you'.[5] Pleased too to make a copy of the letter before delivering it, which was sent on to Thurloe and may well have influenced Cromwell next year to dispense with a jury and set up a High Court of Justice.

What had Slingsby so far said or done? All our information is based on the reports Colonel Smith made to Cromwell and Thurloe, and the subsequent statements of the three officers, Waterhouse, Overton and Thompson, which are likely to be prejudicial. According to Waterhouse Slingsby's son, Henry, had, when they were out hunting in December of '57, given him a book with his father's compliments which he slipped in his pocket and looked at later on. In it he found a piece of paper with a message asking whether Robert Gardiner (probably a brother of that Captain Thomas Gardiner arrested for carrying loaded pistols at Hampton Court) had approached him about serving the king.[6] 'Tell me this', it went on, 'and I will tell you strange things. My son hath engaged not to look into this, going or coming. I will be faithful to you'.[7] Acting on Colonel Smith's orders he went to see Slingsby who took him to the window and 'hugged and embraced' him and asked if Gardiner really had approached him. To which he replied that he had heard Gardiner 'say something in a ranting manner, but not to much purpose'. Slingsby had then told him that if he could secure the South Blockhouse for the king, fifty to one hundred men would march in from Paull by night to assist him and then master the town. A week later he was given the book again with another message offering him, 'if the match goe on, £5000 in land or money, here or elsewhere'. Slingsby, interviewed, had said that once the South Block-house were secured he would 'in a little time bring an army to besiege Hull'. Five or six regiments and an unnamed Colonel were mentioned as well as the 8000 troops, furnished by the King of Spain and led by the Duke of York. Soon after this a third message was sent: 'If the Governor will send for me I will give bond for my peacable living. Give me a peice and I will give you twenty for it if I do not procure you a commission for the government of the South Block-house'.

So much for Waterhouse's statement.[8] Overton, when examined, said that Slingsby, for whom he was responsible, 'thought him the strictest man alive with prisoners' and to avoid having his man searched for letters he now put them 'in a purse with money for his laundress which she carryed into the town and sent them away'. Slingsby had questioned him about the sally-port, by which some prisoners had been planning to escape till they were discovered – where it was and how it entered the Castle and whether he would be able to let 40 men in that way – and had offered him £100 in gratuities to those of his men who helped to effect this, as well as sufficient money to provision the Castle from sources he had in the country. Slingsby had also reminded him of the King's promise of £5000 'to any that assisted him when he first came to kiss his mother earth' and of his request that 'if he should land at Hedon or Fetty[9] or within 2 or 3 miles he would not shoot great bullets at his men as they were landing'. One of those detailed to lead the landings might have been Marmaduke Darcy – 'Duke Dassy' – who had once asked Slingsby what condition Hull was in. In reply Slingsby had quoted Ned Chapman's words to his son, Henry, over dinner one night – that the townspeople could deal with the garrison any day – and had then asked Overton what he thought, to which Overton had guardedly replied that he knew Chapman 'was not for the soldiers'.

Knowing that Lieutenant Thompson was friendly with young Henry and others disaffected to Cromwell the Governor had tried to use him to discover more than the

Achievement of arms of Sir Henry the Elder, displaying fourteen coats with the quartered Vavasour shield in pretence. The Esquire's helmet shows that, unless the painter made a mistake, the glass was stained before Sir Henry's knighthood in 1602. *(By permission of the headmaster of Redhouse Preparatory School.)* *Photograph by W. Farmsworth*

Newburgh Priory in the 17th century. Founded c.1150 by Augustinian Canons who built the imposing central porch to commemorate the visit of Margaret Tudor on her way to Scotland to marry James IV, it was given by Henry VIII to his chaplain, Dr. Anthony Belasyse at the Dissolution. In the background are the Isle and the Hambleton Hills other two officers had been able to, but had not 'found him forward in that worke. He hath not carryed himself well nor honestly, having had private discourse severall times with Sir Henry . . . and did not discover anything of it to mee till I drew it from him'.[10] Nevertheless it was hoped that his evidence might be of some use.

So far Slingsby had uttered only treasonable words, but committed no treasonable act, and until he did so the business could not 'ripen'. But on 2 April the Governor reported: 'This evening Major Waterhouse hath received a commission of Sir Henry Slingsby under the hand and seal of Charles Stuart, in the presence of Captain Overton, which I have inclosed in this letter. I suppose now there will be full and convictive evidence against him and therefore, if His Highness shall think fitt, I will speedily send him up to London by a party of troops, with the Major and Captain Overton'.[11] But this could not be till Overton, confined to his room 'very ill and lame' was fit to travel. In the meantime the Major would try 'to get alight of' a list of 300 counterfeit names which Slingsby had said he possessed. A week later the Governor reported that although Overton was still lame, he was trying to find out more about the business; 'but I fear I shall not lay hold of Gardiner. I cannot heare he is in these partes. He was lately in Flanders I am informed. If he comes into this country I think I shall be sure of him'.[12]

About the same time as this letter was written Slingsby was allowed a visit from his nephew, Robert Stapylton, ostensibly to discuss the settlement of property on his eldest son, Thomas, soon to be married to the step-daughter of Sir Orlando Bridgman, one of the Keepers of the Great Seal — and another Queensman. Overton must have been present for he reported 'some unhandsome expressions which Stapylton delivered to Slingsby.'[13] He wrote these down on a piece of paper which he gave to the Governor who sent it on to Cromwell with the comment that he was sorry that 'any pretending to religion and to good men should give Your Highness' most malicious enemyes such cause of rejoycing as I perceave the wordes mentioned in the inclosed paper hath done'.[14] Whatever Stapylton had said is less important than what he did for, realising the danger his uncle was in, he set off for London where he and his wife went straight to Thomas's lodgings and told him about the delivery of the commission. There was no time to be lost. Thomas instructed his servant, Sanderson, who had been present at the interview, to make all speed to Hull and warn his father that unless he contrived to escape he would almost certainly be sent up to London. Sanderson reached Hull and delivered this message, and Slingsby at once dispatched his servant, John Jefferson, to an ex-officer of the royalist army, Lieutenant William Smith, at Cawood, to ask him for two trusty men who could be 'listed as soldiers' and help him to escape. Smith sent one young man, Gawen Pollard, late Cornet of Horse, by return and promised to follow himself. Pollard was allowed to see Slingsby in private, and was then taken by Jefferson to quarters in the town.[15]

1 TSP VI, 777.
2 TSP VI, 781.
3 TSP VI, 780–1.
4 TSP VI, 870.
5 TSP VII, 125.
6 Underdown, 208.
7 TSP VII, 124.
8 TSP VII, 122–3.
9 There is no such place as Fetty. What may have been meant is Fleet, the harbour at the mouth of Hedon Haven, $5\frac{1}{2}$ miles east of Hull.
10 TSP VII, 127.
11 TSP VII, 46.
12 TSP VII, 65.
13 TSP VII, 127.
14 TSP VII, 65.
15 TSP VII, 112.

Chapter sixteen

1658

ALL THE WELL-WORN METHODS of escape must have been urgently discussed – and dismissed as being too difficult to attempt at such short notice. The best chance might have been a rescue at some favourable point on the way up to London, by no means an impossibility in those days of simmering revolt, but involving the risk that the prisoner might himself be shot on the first hint of danger.

If any plan was made – and the three men, Sanderson, Jefferson and Pollard were dumb, deaf and blind as the proverbial monkeys – it was taken out of their hands by the decision to send Slingsby up by sea, the safest and, with favourable winds, the quickest way. As the ship carrying him and his accusers put out with the tide and sailed down the Humber many watching it from the Castle would have recalled the fate of the Hothams who had gone the same way in the 'Hercules' to the Tower.[1] Perhaps Slingsby himself did, though he was not to know that Waterhouse had with him that incriminating list of pseudonyms which he had found in his room.[2]

The news of his being sent up for trial shocked the Court abroad. Joseph Jane writing to his father-in-law, Secretary Nicholas, said : 'Of all the gentlemen of the king's party I should least have suspected Sir Henry Slingsby for that danger, being a melancholy man and, as I knew him in Parliament, reserved and inactive, but I doubt he has been drawn in'.[3] There were two other prisoners in the Tower awaiting trial by the same court – Mordaunt and Hewitt, both arrested for their activities in the Surrey rising planned for this year. How Slingsby and Hewitt were treated is not known. But for the three weeks before the trial an officer and a private soldier were locked in, day and night, with Mordaunt and his young wife, while two keepers, each with different keys, kept guard outside. Only two days before the trial was he allowed pen and ink, and on the night before it he sat up late preparing his defence, only to be roused, when he had gone to bed, by the Captain doing his rounds, and made to answer questions.[4]

Slingsby and Hewitt, though they never met in the Tower, had been allowed to correspond with each other and both had agreed to question the validity of the court and demand counsel. Hewitt's legal adviser prepared for him a plea which covered $6\frac{1}{2}$ pages of close print, full of legal precedents going back to the reign of Richard II. But Cromwell was determined that there should be no repetition of the leniency shown to the '55 conspirators. He rejected Whitelocke's advice that they should be tried in the ordinary course of trial at the common law, 'being too much in love with the new way', as Whitelocke said, 'which he thought to be the more effectual and would more terrify the offenders'.[5] So he set up a High Court of Justice and nominated forty commissioners of the Seal and the Treasury to sit on it. Whitelocke himself refused to sit.

The trial had been fixed for Tuesday 25 May. That morning Slingsby and Hewitt with their guard had to wait for an hour in the cold at the Watergate of the Tower for Mordaunt;[6] and when he at last appeared, led by the hand by Captain Foster (who had been in charge of the firing squad that shot Lucas and Lisle at Colchester) the guard commander had some harsh things to say about his laziness. He apologized to his fellow-prisoners who, when they saw his face, swollen with an abscess 'of which he had likely died,' readily forgave him. Not so Captain Foster who exclaimed for all to hear that he 'could not blame his story, for never man went out to trial so sure to lose his head'. This stung Mordaunt to ask if he were to be one of their judges and Foster retaliated by laying a hundred to one against his acquittal. The shivering party then embarked and were rowed the mile upstream to Westminster.

'There were thousands of witnesses', writes T. W., 'and Westminster Hall scarce ever so thronged'. Hewitt would have been a sufficient draw by himself for he had 'so sweet a voice and so comely his presence and behaviour that as many came to hear him read prayers as afterwards came to hear him preach'.[7] The King's Bench, where the trial was to take place, was at the upper end of the Hall and here, under royalist colours captured in the war, were seated the forty judges in their scarlet, and the Lord President in his purple robes. This was Lisle, one of Bradshaw's assistants at the trial of Charles I.

Slingsby was first called to the bar and the charge of high treason read by the Attorney General. This stated that he, 'at divers times since October 10th 1655 and before April 30th 1658 as a false traytor and enemy to His Highness Oliver Lord Protector of these Nations, together with one Robert Gardiner and Edward Chapman, and with one William Smith and divers others, did traiterously, advisedly and maliciously combine together . . . to betray and yeild up the Garrison of Hull unto Charles Stuart, eldest son of the late King Charles, now an enemy to this commonwealth ; and that he had likewise tried to stir up mutinies in the garrison and withdraw Ralph Waterhouse, John Overton and George Thompson, Officers of the same, from their obedience to His Highness . . . promising to them rewards and summs of money to joyn with him in the treason aforesaid' ; and that he had corresponded with Charles Stuart and given Waterhouse a commission from Charles appointing him Governor of the Castle.

To this charge Slingsby refused to plead guilty or not guilty, and desired to have counsel assigned him and be tried by jury according to the law of the land. 'We here are all your Jury as well as your Judges', said the President. 'We are the number of two or three juries and your jury is well known, for they are chosen by Parliament ; you are to plead to your indictment'. To Slingsby's question as to whether there could be any conviction 'unless it be by confession' the Lord President replied that if he had read the Act of Parliament it would have told him, for 'it speaks

145

of examination of witnesses, of confession and answer, and of your default, and if you do not plead to it, will be very penal for you'. Slingsby then objected that he was being illegally deprived of taking exception to any member of the jury, who were also his judges, but was told that the court had been appointed by parliament, of which he was still a member even though he was a prisoner, to whose acts the whole people of England must submit. If he had 'any particular exception to any man, he might make it'. There were forty Commissioners and all of them, as Slingsby objected, were his enemies who had sequestered and sold his estates because he would not compound, and had denied him the Act of Oblivion.[8] So it was useless to take exception to any one of them. After further remonstrances he pleaded Not Guilty. The Attorney General thereupon said that, the charge and plea having been heard, it rested with the Commissioners to prove the prisoner guilty; adding that if justice had been done to him in '55 at York he would not now be here before them. Mercy, rather than justice, had then prevailed; yet ever since then he had not ceased 'to interpose on the behalf of Charles Stuart and to withdraw the faithfull officers of the garrison to betray their trust' by offering them money and preferment.

The witnesses were then called, first Major Waterhouse, whose evidence was much the same as that given in his statement. The commission Slingsby was alleged to have given him was then read out. It was subscribed 'Given at Bruges March 12 1657' but Slingsby denied that it was the same one he had given, which was originally dated April 12, but on Waterhouse's request he had scraped out April and substituted March. Both Waterhouse and Overton swore, however, that it was the same and the matter was dropped. Waterhouse then read out the letter from Charles which Walters had delivered. Concluding his evidence he said that Overton was to have been his Deputy Governor and that Slingsby had had 'good hopes' that Colonel Smith would also accept a commission. At this Slingsby interposed 'This which is here spoken in seriousness was then spoke in mirth, a meer discourse as those that are in good fellowship may have, and what I said or did was but in jest'; which drew

146

from the President 'There ought to be no good fellowship in treason'.

Overton's evidence varied little from his original statement and Slingsby was asked if he had anything to say. 'I see I am trepanned by these two fellows', he replied. 'They have said that seriously against me which was spoken in mirth between us; I never sought them, but they me; the commission was procured by no intercourse with any persons beyond the seas, but a blank one which I had for four years together. Nor had I any correspondence beyond the sea to carry on my design here'. This commission would have been one of those issued by Rochester.

Thompson in his evidence said he had been ordered by Waterhouse to visit Slingsby on 16 April and the next day had asked him to walk on the leads where Slingsby had hugged him and said 'he had a great deal of confidence' in him, and that he would receive notice of the date the king was expected to come. 'I confess such like discourses', interjected Slingsby, 'but Waterhouse asked me to speak to Thompson to try whether he would be an assistant, but I told him I would not lest he should not accept, and then turn him out of his place. Waterhouse pressed me to go to Thompson, and invited us to his house to dinner; after dinner he spoke to Thompson to go with me on the leads to shew me the guns; we walked about and came down again. Then said Waterhouse to me "Did you not speak to Thompson?" I said not. "You had a good opportunity" said he. At last Thompson came to me and I had some discourse with him about it'.

After the charge, plea and evidence had been summed up the Attorney General, in his address, stressed the strategic importance of Hull, 'the most considerable place in England for Charles Stuart's design', and concluded: 'My Lord, I pitty this Gentleman that those grey hairs should thus go to the grave. I have no more to say but crave the justice of this court'.

The court now adjourned for private debate in the Painted Chamber and the prisoner was taken away, back to the Tower by water. As the boat drew away from Westminster Stairs, and the roofs and turrets of Westminster

Hall and the Painted Chamber, where the Commissioners were debating his case, receded Slingsby, like all those others who had made the same journey under the shadow of the axe, must have been calculating his chances.

Hewitt likewise questioned the validity of the court and refused to plead, protesting that he was 'better acquainted with a pulpit than a bar'.[9] The chief witness against him was John Stapley of Sussex who had originally promised to raise 500 horse and been given a commission in which Hewitt had inserted his name – Sir John Stapley Bart. – this title being one of the rewards he had demanded, together with a pardon for his father who had been a regicide. Hewitt's refusal to plead caused the Commissioners to lose all patience and cry 'Take him away! Take him away!' One eye-witness remarked that his speech 'seemed to be starched on purpose for the lady spectators, towards whom he often turned on each side'.

When Mordaunt's turn came he, like the other two, challenged the legality of the court and kept his hat on till the Sergeant came to remove it, when he threw it away. He too was sent back to the Tower. But his beautiful, wealthy and vivacious wife used her multiple charms to bribe some of the judges, from whom she received a two fold message – that unless her husband stopped arguing and agreed to plead they could do nothing to help him; and that his chief danger lay in the second witness, Colonel Henry Mallory. Next day when the trial was resumed a note was handed to the President who passed it on to the Lieutenant of the Tower, who in turn passed it to Mordaunt. It was from his wife and contained the urgent message: 'For God's sake plead! Plead for my sake and stand disputing it no longer!' He at once changed his tactics, showing that 'he knew how to speak as well as how to attempt or die'. That night Mallory found in his room in the Tower a suit, cloak and breeches with £50 in the pocket and the address of a house in Blackfriars to go to. Next morning, as he was being brought into Westminster Hall he gave his guard the slip, mingled with the crowd and escaped. When his name was called and he could not be found, the court adjourned, after ordering a hue-and-cry.[10]

On Thursday 27 May the court met again in the Painted Chamber, discussed the three cases for a couple of hours, and adjourned once more till Tuesday, 1 June, for further consideration, after which the prisoners were told they would hear their sentences on the next day. But it was not until 4 p.m., after six hours of discussion, that they were summoned to Westminster Hall. Slingsby was first called and asked if he had any more objections to the court's now pronouncing judgment on him. He appealed once more for trial by jury but was told by the President 'this is not a time for pleading. Therefore I must require your silence and hear me a few words'. In those few words he first likened Slingsby's hardness of heart to that of the Egyptians who persecuted the Israelites, in spite of the many signs and wonders by which God had declared himself on the side of the Israelites, 'by a series of wonderful Providences so many years together against that very party who are still hatching treason and rebellions among us. You cannot chuse but see that the Lord fights against you, that the stars in their courses fight against you, and yet you will not see, you will not confess until destruction overtakes you . . . Sir, if the signal and wonderful Providences of God will not deter you, yet methinks National considerations should deter you from such a treason as this. Charles Stuart is in confederacy with Spain against England, he is in confederacy with that great Popish interest. Is it imaginable that an Englishman, that a Protestant, should assist such a confederacy as this? Yet that which is not imaginable in itself is here clearly and evidently proved before us . . . What said you to the proof? You confessed upon the matter all, in effect all; but only some things you said by way of excuse, and I shall truly relate them all'. Then, as Slignsby said in a letter to a friend, the President turned with a supercilious smile and continued : 'All you did, you told us was but in jest. What, Sir, if those discontented English that complied with Spain in Queen Elizabeth's days in '88 had said they had been in jest, what would you have thought of that? What if those Jesuited Papists that would have blown up Parliament upon the 5th of November with barrels of gunpowder, had said that they had brought in those barrels in jest, what would you have thought of it? Sir Harry, you have jested yourself fairly out of your fame, estate, and now according to the merit of your cause very like to jest yourself into a grave to your lasting dishonour. Sir, be not deceived. As a man sows, so shall he reap. You have sowed treason and rebellion and now you are to reap the fruit'.

After complimenting 'the prudent and faithfull Governor of Hull, Colonel Smith' and those 'worthy and faithfull commanders' Waterhouse, Overton and Thompson, who had 'carried themselves in this business like the men of understanding that Solomon speaks of' (though according to Shaw they were not above cheating the prisoners at cards), he returned to his anti-papal theme, asking what would have become of the protestant interest in England, Scotland and Ireland if Slingsby had had his will and 'Charles Stuart had come in. If you had but time (but the Lord knows you have not time) to look over the records of England and the Declarations of Parliament since 1640 it would tell you what Family it was that betrayed the protestant interest in France when Rochel was taken; what Family it was that betrayed the Protestant interest in Germany and in the Palatinate when a peace was made with Spain without consent of Parliament. What could you think of that Family that did tolerate popery for a match with Spain?

And now, Sir, but one word more to you as you are an Englishman, I beseech you consider what would have become of this nation if you had had your will. You would have brought on a new Civil War upon England at the least. I cannot think of a new Civil War but I think of desolation upon desolation to this poor nation. And now let me add this word to these two Gentlemen. Sirs, when I have done speaking, I shall never have done praying for you, as long as you are alive. That is the last thing I must say to you. And now let the judgment of the court be read'.

1 In July 1643 the Hothams were taken by sea to London in the 'Hercules'.
2 TSP VII, 98.
3 CSPD 1658–9, 21.
4 'The Trial of Mr. Mordaunt – or the Pretended High Court of Justice in Westminster Hall, 1 and 2 June 1658' by T. W. (British Museum G.4964)
5 Whitelocke, Memorials.
6 'The Trial of Mr. Mordaunt etc.' by T. W.
7 D. Lloyd, Memoirs.
8 The Act of Oblivion of 24 February 1652 pardoned all guilty of treasons and felonies against the State committed before the date of the battle of Worcester, 3 September, 1651. But there were many exceptions, of which Slingsby was one. EHR 1937, 637.
9 Cobbett, State Trials, 885.
10 TSP VII, 220.
   Clarendon XV, 97.

Chapter Seventeen

1658

THE SENTENCE, read by the Clerk, ran: 'That the said Sir Henry Slingsby as a false traytor to his said Highness Lord Protector and this Commonwealth shall be conveyed back to the Tower of London, and from thence through the middle of the City of London, directly shall be brought unto the Gallows of Tibourn and upon the said Gallows shall be hanged, and being alive shall be cut down to the ground, and his entrails taken out of his belly and, he living, be burnt before him ; and that his head shall be cut off and that his body shall be divided into four quarters'.

Hewitt, who followed him to the bar, received a like sentence, the petition permitting him to plead (which his wife, then with child, had spent a whole night on her knees imploring him to sign) having been rejected by the Court.[1] Mordaunt was acquitted, saved by Mallory's absence and by the sudden illness of Colonel Pride (of Pride's Purge notoriety), one of the judges who had resolved to condemn him but returned only in time to hear the President, faced with a vote of nineteen all, give his casting vote in the prisoner's favour. When Mallory was later recaptured Cromwell demanded a retrial, but bowed to public opinion, though he did not release Mordaunt for several months. As soon as he was released 'it was very few days before he embarked himself as frankly in the king's service as before, and with more success'.[2]

The crowds of spectators had had their money's worth. They had heard Mordaunt's spirited defence and witnessed his dramatic acquittal; they had revelled in the impassioned oratory of Dr. Hewitt whom Cromwell had once described as 'a flaming torch in the midst of a sheaf of corn;'[3] and perhaps marvelled at the stoicism of the northerner, Slingsby, who later admitted his slowness in reply and personal defence, 'being confident no words could have been spoken by me at my arraignment that would have been construed seasonable, so highly was the Presidential Court pre-possessed against me'.

Cromwell's daughters, Mary Fauconberg and Elizabeth Claypole, both during the trial and after sentence, pleaded unceasingly for the lives of the two men. Fauconberg, in desperation, tried to get the French ambassador to enlist the aid of Louis XIV, but all in vain. The most Cromwell would grant was the mitigation of the sentence to beheading, and postponement of the date from Saturday to the following Tuesday. This gave the condemned men five days in which to prepare themselves, a task made easier, writes Slingsby, by 'the gentle demean and civilities of our Lieutenant; and by his command of the soldiers modest carryage towards us, in our private devotions and other holy duties. Which pious Office, as it conduceth much to our peace, so it cannot but redound highly to the Commander's honour'.

There was little to conduce to Cromwell's peace of mind in those days. He had dissolved a parliament that would not vote him money, and the army had not been paid for six months. He was ill and went in daily fear of his life, never disclosing which route his coach would follow till he was in it, and even then proceeding under heavy guard.[4] He had suffered, and was suffering, much personal sorrow. His youngest daughter's husband, young Rich, had died early in the year within three months of the marriage. His favourite daughter, Elizabeth, whose little son Oliver had recently died, was desperately ill and 'raving in a most lamentable manner' over Hewitt's impending death. There were no comfortable words for him in his own home.

For the spiritual comfort of the two prisoners the Commissioners ordered that Dr. Reynolds, Mr Caryl, Mr Calamy and Mr Manton should be sent to prepare them for death. A more welcome visitor would have been Slingsby's cousin, another Henry Slingsby, a waggish-looking man with a squint who was a great friend of Evelyn, a lover of music and the arts, and a senior official of the Royal Mint which was then in the Tower. He is almost certainly the Henry Slingsby who sent weekly reports on the political situation to Hyde at the Hague, from 1658 to 1660, writing in a numerical cipher and in a disguised hand, under the pseudonym of 'Samborne'.[5]

But to Slingsby, when his hours were numbered as irrevocably as the tides that ebbed and flowed below the barred window, the most precious, though agonising, visits must have been those of his sons and daughter. This comes out in that 'Father's Legacy to his Sons' which reflects what had gone on in his mind during those years of imprisonment, and his earnest desire to guide his children – 'My tender Ones, for never were children more dear to a Father' – after he was gone. 'But my Preamble must not be long', he writes, 'seeing the definite sentence of death hath limitted my time so short. My beginning shall receive life from Him from whom we all derive our beginning whom you are above all things to fear, and that with no servile but filial fear, not so much for fear of punishment or hope of reward as out of pure zeal and cordial love to his Sacred Majesty, who will recompense our momentary sufferings with crowns of immortal glory, and cloath our constancy with incorruptible robes of beauty. But no combat, no conquest; you are to fight a good fight before your warfare becomes a triumph . . . I hold him a weak-hearted soldier that faints under the conduct of such a Commander, who patiently died for our sins and victoriously rose for our justification', words that reflect his own constant loyalty to the lost cause of that earthly Majesty which would one day be triumphant.

Long imprisonment and solitude have been, he says, 'a place of infinite improvement, to recollect myself, and seriously to meditate how my too near and familiar society with the world (tho' never deeply drenched in it) was the high way to procure a divorce from God . . . This was the mirror that flattered not'. Captivity had brought him more benefit than all his 'forepast liberty. For before I knew not what it was to wrastle with myself, till restraint (an usefull, though unwelcome Messenger) brought me to a due and exact consideration of myself'. Visiting friends and relatives were 'daily contriving new, but affectionate, ways how to call me from myself and reduce my thoughts to a more familiar converse with the world', but they succeeded only when they got him to reflect on the youth and inexperience of his children. Reading between the lines there appears to have been some pretty heated discussion here, and all the old arguments used once before, when his estates were threatened with confiscation, must have come up again. Nevertheless what his 'constancy (or what others termed pertinacy) of opinion would not assent to the amicable care of faithful Trustees effected . . . This quieted my thoughts and brought me again to myself. As one in a safe harbour, I began to recal to mind those divine contemplations which my late converse with secular occasions had so prejudicially estranged from me . . . And I concluded my review of these, how all things were vanity, save only to please God, and to serve him. Make this your anchor-hold, and you may sail safely. For it is the high estimate that men set upon this world, captives their affections, making them heavily leave what they did so heartily love'.

He now takes 'a turn or two in the Temple' but, unlike his father, proposes no 'rules of religion' to his children except to warn them against 'Novellisme, whose pernicious seed has spread so many dangerous Sects, Schismes and Heresies, and begotten so many breaches and fearful rents in the Church as it is above the compass of human wisdom to make up the decays of so disjointed a fabrick'. Place-hunting theologians, 'profest champions for broaching error and sedition', have been most guilty of 'imbroiling the quiet of the Church and exposing the long-continued unity which she formerly enjoyed to those fatal miseries of endless divisions; which broke forth into national quarrels and such implacable hostility as the Church became a constant Patient, but no hand so inclinable to pity as to apply to her bleeding wounds a timely remedy'. He, if anyone, could write feelingly about these quarrels as he recalled those powerful Earls of Northumberland plotting to restore Catholicism, and the many close friends and relatives – anglican, puritan, presbyterian – with whom and against whom he had fought. But his sons, he says, 'have learned better things; relie then on those just and orthodoxicall Principles which retain in them that powerful efficacy, as they will teach you how to believe and how to live. Men have nothing to give but what they receive, and what I have received I shall here by advice freely communicate unto you'.

His first piece of advice is to submit themselves to their superiors in all things lawful, which he himself is perforce about to do. 'The crime wherewith I stood charged was Treason, which my conscience dictated to me bare the cognizance of Loyalty. To which principle, as I was nursed in it, so I mean to death to continue a constant Professor of it'. Many had thought him wrong in this, and in refusing to compound, and in appealing against the legality of the High Court. 'Though I was, as some thought, slow in my reply and personal defence at the barr, may it stand with the patience of good men to hear the modest Apology which I here recommend to their perusal after my death . . . Words spoken in season retain precious resemblances; but I am confident no words could have been spoken by me at my arraignment that would have been construed seasonable, so highly was the Presidential Court prepossessed against me. My defence shall be short, dissecting itself into two particulars'.

Firstly, he says, he was bound by conscience which would give him no peace if checked – 'there was in it either a continual feast to cheer me, or a cloud of witnesses to condemn me'. His Oath of Allegiance was sustained 'by an inviolable tie of religious love', against which all 'sinewy arguments to decline my opinion during my several places of imprisonment' had failed. Even his worst enemies, who called his constancy contumacy, could hardly interpret it otherwise than 'an errour of love, but no love of errour, being so integriously grounded that it admitted no alloy or mixture with by-respects or self interests'.

His second 'motive', which echoed the first, was 'resolution for Loyalty' against which he has heard, and read, the arguments of sundry anti-monarchical authors (of whom he mentions Paraeus, Zwinglius and Buchanan – but not his own nephew, Slingsby Bethell); but he dismisses these as 'colourable disguises, meerly to catch and circumvent us, being afterwards, to expedite our dispatch, produced as evidence against us', and he commands his sons 'not to look upon these Agents with a vindictive eye. Your father has forgiven them, do you the like . . . We cannot share in a Crown if we have no part in the Cross. And blessed be his name that has armed my weakness with this resolution, preparing in me a mind no less ready to bear than justice was to inflict. My actions, by God's assistance, shall in this approaching hour of my suffering express it, though I shall appear slow in the elegancy or flourish of words (for I never profest myself an orator neither indeed should I hold such a dress suitable to any one going to his death).'

He goes on to stress 'one particular, which infinitely concerns you; and that is your choice of company. Good acquaintance will improve both your knowledge and demean, whereas our debauched Gallantry (the greatest Imposter of youth) will by their society quickly deprave you. Be tender therefore of your Honour; beware with whom you consort, be known to many, but familiar with few'. He then addresses each in turn. To Tom, 'the immediate hope of my House, whose course has been hitherto approvable, enabled by generous education abroad and imitable examples at home', he has much to say which this young man must have felt would take a lot of living up to – except for the summing up: 'express yourself moderate in arguements of dispute, close in your counsels and discreet in your discourse'. For Harry who, 'though younger, has been ever dear and near my heart since thine infancy, thine innocence has here for a season been a sufferer with thy Father [an allusion to their companionship during his imprisonment in Hull]; but let it not grieve thee to partake with him who doth so truly tender thee . . . I shall sacrifice my life freely, as one subject to an assumed Authority; be it their goodness to spare thine innocence. I hope my blood may sufficiently expiate the grandeur of my crime, without farther revenge'. The estates that are left him should be competent for a younger brother; 'if your estate be not sufficient for you, be sufficient for your estate. Return my blessing to your sister, my dear Bab, whose unblemished fame has conferred a high additament to my comfort, and incomparably revived me in this my irrevocable sentence to the scaffold, and tell her from a dying Father that she needs no other example than her vertuous Mother for her Directory, in whose steps I am confident she will walk religiously. Her modest and blameless demean can promise nothing less.

And now my dear Ones, as my desire is that you should in this last Legacy of my Love and parental duty remember me, so my request is that neither you nor any of my relations suffer that memory they retain of me to be accompanied with immoderate grief. After a troublesome voyage encountered with many cross winds and adverse billows, I am now arriving in a safe Harbour: and I hope without touch of Dishonour.

As for Death, though it appear terrible to all flesh, I have long expected it, and by a conscientious consequence prepared me for it. And to make it more familiar to me, before I was called up to this City, I made my coffin my companion, that I might with more resolution look Death in the face whensoever it should assault me. An hatchet to a weak spirit may present more fear, but a fever to a patient more pain'.

As the time for his execution drew nearer he penned those 'Devotionall Addresses' which begin with six lines of verse:

Death's Doom to sensual ears sad tidings brings
For death's the King of fears, and fear of Kings;
But to a mind resigned, a welcome Guest,
And only convoy to the Port of Rest;
A freer from restraint, wherein I long
Estranged from earth's content, sing Sion's Song.

Then follow sixty exhortations of varying length, culled one imagines from his Commonplace Book. And the 'Additional Instructions privately delivered before his coming to Tower-hill', which he may well have scribbled as he waited for the summons. Almost the last words he wrote were 'Continue firm in brotherly unity; as you are near in blood, be dear in affection'.

Though he besought them 'Make every day of your lives a promising passage to your Native Country', whither he himself was now 'breathing homeward', his thoughts must often have turned to that earthly home, Redhouse, he was leaving, passing in memory from one well-remembered room to another, reliving his life there before and after the war; kneeling in the chapel, scene of so many family events, now wrapt in its own light and peace; looking from the terrace over ripening cornfields and buttercup meadows to the twin towers of York Minster gleaming on the skyline; or standing by the wood to gaze once more at the blue hills where Barbara came from, and then at Redhouse itself, now glowing in June sunshine, doors and windows wide open to welcome the traveller home.

The official report of the execution reads: 'At about eleven o'clock Sir Henry Slingsby was brought from the Tower to the scaffold on Tower Hill, whither being come hee fell upon his knees and for a short time prayed privately. Then standing up, he did in a short speech, and with a very low voice, address himself to that noble Gentleman Mr Sheriff Robinson, telling him that what he had to say he would speak to him; which was to this purpose: that he had received a sentence to die upon account of his endeavouring to betray the Garrison of Hull; but all that he did in that business he was drawn into by others; that the Officers of that Garrison did believe he had some greater designe in hand, and therefore they would needs pump him to the bottom. But what he spoke to them in private was brought into evidence against him. He likewise said that he did no more than any person would have done that was so brought on; and that he had made many applications (by his friends) for a reprieve, but found His Highness was inexorable. He did confess he did deliver a commission (as it was charged against him) but said that it was an old commission, and what he meant was well known to himself; but what construction others had made of it might appear by his present condition. He discovered little sense of sorrow or fear of death, but said he was ready to submit. He was to die, as he expressed himself exultingly on the scaffold, for being

159

an honest man, of which he was very glad, but sorry only that it was not for some more effectual service to His Majesty. He took off a scarf-ring from his band-string with, instead of a seal ingraven, had a picture of the late King exactly done and, giving it to a gentleman that stood by, said "Pray, Sir, give this to Harry". Then he addressed himself to private prayer again for a short time; then laid his head upon the block and at the signe given the Executioner severed his head from his body at one blow; and his friends put his body into a coffin and removed it into a close coach, prepared near the place'.

He had taken with him to the scaffold two devotional books – Melanchton's 'Chronicum Absolutissimum' which had belonged to his grandfather, Francis, and Augustine's 'Meditations', with Arthur Capel's name in it and the inscription 'To my very lovinge friend Henry Slingesbie', a book Capel had perhaps taken with him to his own execution eight years before in Westminster Palace Yard.[6] The white shirt he was wearing at the time is still preserved and shows a cut of the axe on the broad collar, and a blood stain.

Hewitt's execution[7] followed immediately, and so were added the last two to those other sixteen sufferers for the royal cause whose portraits, engraved by Vertue, were grouped, in a composite picture, round that of Charles I and likened, in the Latin couplets at the base, to so many red suns setting, to rise again in golden light.[8] That of Slingsby shows him 'in prison, dressed in black, a turnover, and with grey hair and a small beard'. His body, 'at the intercession of his friends, was permitted by the Usurper to be privately carried down into Yorkshire, there to be interred in the burial place of his ancestors; which was done with all decent solemnity' in the Slingsby Chapel in Knaresborough Church. His tombstone is a slab of black marble from the rock-cut chapel of St. Robert the Hermit (said to have covered the saint's tomb), and lies on the floor of the chapel to the west of the elaborate altar-tomb of his grandparents, Francis and Mary, who recline in effigy, he in complete armour with the Slingsby lion at foot, she robed and with hair combed back, with the Percy crescent at foot. Looking down from the north wall is the chill shrouded figure of his father, proclaiming 'All is vanity;' and in a niche on the opposite wall stands his uncle, Sir William, more comfortably clad and less reproachful of this world. A recent restoration of the chapel revealed the headless remains of the cavalier.

Did he deserve to die? Colonel Ludlow, a staunch parliamentarian, thought not and said so forcibly writing in his Memoirs[9] that Slingsby 'had had very hard measure. For it appeared that he was a prisoner at the time when he was charged to have practised against the government; that he was a declared enemy and therefore by the laws of war free to make any such attempt; besides it was alledged that the persons whom he was accused to have corrupted had trepand him by their promises to serve the King in delivering Hull, if he would give them a commission to act for him, which commission was an old one that had long lain by him. But all this not being thought sufficient to excuse him he was adjudged to die'. A modern historian writes:[10] 'His case stands out as one of the worst examples of the distasteful business of trepanning during the entire Protectorate ... He was led on until the proofs of his treason were legally complete. The whole process was controlled at every stage by Cromwell and Thurloe'. Whitelocke, who questioned the legality of the High Court of Justice which Cromwell set up, refused to sit on it as one of the Commissioners.

What Cromwell's innermost thoughts were we shall never know. In August, two months after the execution, his much-loved daughter Elizabeth, by whose bedside he would sit, neglecting all public business, died still 'upbraiding him with the blood he had spilt', which remonstrance it was said 'sunk deep into his mind and it was strongly suspected that his conscience took alarm and was never at rest from that moment'.[11] His object had been to make an example of these three men, victims for the nobility, the clergy and the gentry and so put an end to all further plots. Whether he would have succeeded, and so perhaps justified the expediency of his decision, it is impossible to judge for within three months of the double execution he himself was dead.

He died on 3 September 1658, during 'the greatest

storm of wind that had ever been known, which overthrew trees and made great wrecks at sea',[12] in one of which Charles Davison, still plotting against him, was drowned in the Channel.[13] Another occurrence, recalled by the superstitious, was a Newsletter report that had appeared two days before the execution 'of the killing of a great whale about 50 foot long in the river near Greenwich, many porpusses being also seen to rise that day above the bridge',[14] which events were now proclaimed as portents like those which preceded the death of Julius Caesar. Mordaunt's caustic comment was 'God who sent Cromwell to us as a scourge for our sins, has now sent him to a hot place for his own'. But Fauconberg, writing to Henry Cromwell in Ireland, said 'My poor wife, I know not what on earth to doe with her; when seemingly quieter she bursts out again into passion that tears her very heart to peices; nor can I blame her, considering what she has lost'.[15] She knew better than most what had been lost, for she knew her brothers.

[1] Clarke Papers III, 153. 'He petitioned His Highness for 20 days' reprieve and if in that time he confessed not matters to meritt his life, then to be executed'.
[2] Clarendon VI, 64.
[3] Cobbett, State Trials, 930–3.
[4] Clarendon XV, 143.
[5] CClSP IV, 148, 162. All the 'Samborne' letters are in the Bodleian and show his original and disguised hand.
[6] Capel had asked for his heart to be buried with Charles I. It was given, in a silver casket, to Charles II who returned it to his son and it was ultimately buried in Capel's tomb in Little Hadham church.
[7] R. Beake, writing to Henry Cromwell, says that Hewitt 'spent much time upon the scaffold, and in a great measure justified himself'. Hobman 'Cromwell's Master Spy', 131. Early next year 'a seditious pamphlet called 'Beheaded, or Dr. Hewitt's Ghost pleading, yea crying for exemplary justice against his late judges and executioners', was printed by Prynne. CClSP IV, 161.
[8] Reproduced in Birkenhead's 'Strafford', 196, from the original in the British Museum.
[9] Ludlow 'Memoirs', i. 606.

10   Underdown, 'Royalist Conspiracy in England', 228.

11   Granger, Biographies, III 33.

12   Clarendon XV, 146.

13   CCISP IV, 71. John Cooper, writing to Hyde 3 September from Antwerp, reports the unsuccessful search for Davison's body, 'but has given direction for notice as soon as it floats and is taken up, for the preservation of the things about him'. As it happened no incriminating papers were found on him.

14   Clarke Papers III, 153.

15   TSP VII, 375.

Chapter Eighteen

1659 – 1660

MARSTON MOOR still lay brooding, among its woods and marshes and whin-covered sandy wastes, on the first two Acts of the drama played there under cover of darkness – the royalist disaster of '44 and the royalist fiasco of '55 – and the wind hissing through the rushes and over the long graves, the bark of fox, the hooting of owls, and the chuckle of the sinuous river that had run red with blood, echoed this sombre theme. But a royalist dawn was slowly breaking. From February of 1659 onwards 'Samborne' was writing to Hyde that parliament would gladly call in the king if it did not fear the army. In April he wrote that 'the King must be in readiness not to lose a day' and that Richard Cromwell was 'little better than a prisoner'. He even put his house in the Strand, Slyngesby House, at Charles's disposal.[1] Then in August came those regional risings, of which all failed. Mordaunt rose in Surrey and barely escaped arrest. Fauconberg cautiously showed himself in York, only to retire without doing anything and be arrested and sent to the Tower.[2] Robert Walters was also arrested on landing in Lincolnshire, and John Belasyse in London. Only Booth put up any show in Cheshire and Lancashire, and 'Samborne' appealed to Hyde to create a diversion – '2000 men to be landed with arms, ammunition and artillery about Norfolk', then denuded of parliamentary forces.[3] But the end was a foregone conclusion, as indeed was the end of all attempts to restore the monarchy by force, and Booth fought in vain. The presbyterian-royalist alliance, however, which

Mordaunt had been striving for, was nearer than ever before. To both parties a restoration seemed the only answer to anarchy. That answer might come from Monck and his army in Scotland.

So it was that the curtain for the third Act of the drama rose on Brian Fairfax, just down from Cambridge, riding in disguise a week before Christmas, 1659, with a verbal message from his uncle, the old Commander-in-Chief, to Monck on the Border, saying he would take the field on New Years Day with such forces as he could collect, and asking Monck to keep an eye on Lambert. The adventures of this young man, who had to ride round by Westmorland to avoid Lambert's army, make a tale in themselves. But the message got through and the messenger returned with Monck's promise to watch Lambert as a cat watches a mouse.[4] Fairfax kept his side of the bargain and, though crippled with gout, evaded the troops sent to seize him and left Nun Appleton in his coach, with an escort of only ten, drove through Lilburne's outposts and met Slingsby's son, Sir Thomas, with fifty men at Arthington. Together they went to the rendezvous on Marston Moor where Colonel Sir Hugh Bethell, the Yorkshire Gentlemen,[5] and the Irish Brigade still in Lambert's army, were drawn up. At the sight of their old Commander the Brigade deserted and came over to him. Sir Philip Monckton,[6] by bold bluffing in York, had persuaded the citizens to let Fairfax enter the city in peace, which he did on 2 January 1660 causing, as 'Samborne' reported, 'so great a mutiny in Lambert's army that Lambert is fled'.[7] Ten days later Monck arrived with his army and, briefed by Fairfax at Nun Appleton, continued his march to London, leaving Bethell and Robert Walters to mop up 'Lambertonian' resistance in York,[8] and Hull unsubdued in his rear since Colonel Overton, reinstated as Governor, said he would deliver it 'only to those who bore the image of Jesus Christ'.[9] On 12 January 'Samborne' reported 'Monck is marching hither with 3000 horse, but his answer is not yet come to the city'.[10] But a month later Barbara Slingsby was able to write to her brother, Sir Thomas, that the night Monck 'declared for a free parliament there was the most universall joy throwout the towne

I ever saw, t'was all the night as light as day with the multiplisity of bonefires',[11] and she advised him to get himself chosen for parliament. Robert Slingsby was already standing as one of the Knights of the Shire for Hertfordshire. 'Samborne' told Hyde it was now safe for him to send his replies direct to his cousin Arthur instead of through the Abbess of Ghent[12] who till now had been acting as a secret forwarding agent. And on 18 May the Parliamentary Commission, headed by Fairfax, sailed to The Hague to invite Charles to take the crown. In Hull Charles was proclaimed by Colonel Fairfax, Lord Fairfax's uncle, to the ringing of bells, thundering of guns and volleys from the soldiers. Effigies of Cromwell and Bradshaw in judges' robes were drawn through the streets, thrown into a tar barrel and then burnt, all this within a year of Slingsby's execution.[13]

But the general rejoicings were marred, against the will of Charles, by the exhumation and hanging in chains at Tyburn of the bodies of Cromwell, Bradshaw and Ireton and the setting up of their heads over Westminster Hall. Cromwell's head, after many vicissitudes, was buried in 1960 in the chapel of Sidney Sussex College where he had spent a year as a Fellow Commoner just before Slingsby went up to Queens'. His body, according to strong local tradition, was secretly brought to Newburgh Priory at the Restoration by his daughter Mary, who used her considerable influence at court to have another body substituted at Tyburn for that of her father. On the door of a sealed room at the top of the house there is an inscription which begins 'In this vault are Cromwell's bones'.

It is less than 20 miles from Newburgh to Knaresborough where Slingsby's headless remains are interred, or to the little church on Bilbrough Hill whence Fairfax liked to survey the wide view and where he is buried. 'In these tragick revolutions of human fortunes ourselves shall be the actors' Slingsby had written. These three, and those thousands of nameless ones who played their last part on Marston Moor, lie within this small triangle of the green Vale of York. Let T. S. Eliot's lines[14] be their requiem:

These men, and those who opposed them
And those whom they opposed
Accept the constitution of silence
And are folded in a single party.

1   CCISP IV, 186, 192.
2   CCISP IV, 462.
3   CCISP IV, 322.
4   HMC VI Report 466; YAJ 1939, 490. Woolrych.
5   YAJ 1883.
    Among the Yorkshire Gentlemen was Miles Stapylton, Robert's youngest brother. His father-in-law, Sir Ingram Hopton, was slain at Winceby after having knocked Cromwell down with the hardest blow he ever received in his life.
6   Monckton Papers 31–44.
7   CCISP IV 516.
8   HMC V Report, 199. As late as 21 April a suspected plot caused Bethell and Robert Walters to search York inns at midnight. They found soldiers in bed, fully armed, their horses saddled and bridled in stables. They were to be aided by 'Lambertonian' townsmen and some of the garrison.
9   YAJ 1939, 499.
10 CCISP IV, 517.
11 Diary, 355–6.
12 CCISP IV 642–3. The Abbess was Mary Knatchbull.
13 Tickell, 514.
14 From 'Little Gidding'.

Epilogue

THE CULMINATION of all royalist hopes came with coronation of Charles II, whom Fairfax mounted for the occasion on a horse bred out of the chestnut mare he had ridden at Naseby. That night 'the city had a light like a glory about it with bonfires' wrote Pepys who, with many another health-drinker, had to admit 'if ever I was foxed it was now'.[1] Those of the regicides who had not escaped were tried under the Presidency of the Lord Chief Baron, Sir Orlando Bridgman, Sir Thomas Slingsby's step-father-in-law. Of the two concerned with this story, Lilburne and Lisle, Lilburne said at his trial 'What I did, I did very innocently, without any intention of murder . . . I never read the laws nor understood the case thoroughly. Upon the day the King was put to death I wept in my chamber and would, if I had had the power, have preserved his life'.[2] He was banished to the Isle of St. Nicholas, Plymouth, where he died five years later. Lisle, who had been one of Bradshaw's assistants at the king's trial and had also sentenced Slingsby, escaped with other regicides to Switzerland where, four years later, he was shot dead by an Irish royalist, on his way to church, in Vevey churchyard.[3] Slingsby Bethell, a fanatical republican, had joined the regicides in Vevey soon after the Restoration and is thought to have been the one to whom Ludlow entrusted the MS of his Memoirs – 'Those many reams of paper he had, whilst grumbling in Switzerland, emptied his galls into' as one critic described them. Bethell ultimately returned to London and in 1680 became its Sheriff, in which office he was castigated by Dryden in 'Absalom and Achitophel' for his parsimony :

Chaste were his cellars, and his shrieval board
The grossness of a city feast abhorred.
His cooks with long disuse their trade forgot,
Cool was his kitchen, though his brains were hot.

Thurloe, elected M.P. for Cambridge soon after Cromwell's death, was charged with high treason at the Restoration, but this was not proceeded with. Though boasting that he had 'a black book which should hang half of those that went for Cavaliers',[4] he had told Morland of his private intention to live in Normandy, not trusting that the king would ever forget 'the blood of Penruddock, Slingsby and Hewitt and others whose deaths he had contrived'.[5] But he, and his system of mail interception, which Morland demonstrated to the King late one night in the G.P.O., were too useful to Charles's government and were carried on till the Great Fire destroyed 'all the machines and utensils belonging to the arts'.[6] So Thurloe lived on in the quiet of Great Milton in Oxfordshire till his death in 1668, when he was buried in Lincoln's Inn.

Of the many whose names recur in Thurloe's State Papers Nic Armorer was rewarded with a Captaincy in the King's Own Footguards in Dublin where he died, in his chair, in 1686.[7] John Cooper, his intrepid friend, became a Carver in the Royal Household. Robert Walters, imprisoned in Hull after his capture in '59, became High Sheriff of Yorkshire the next year and in '61 was serving as Captain of the King's Regiment of Guards in Dunkirk. Marmaduke Langdale, though created Lord Langdale of Holme, had been ruined by the wars in which he had spent £160,000, and was too poor to attend the coronation. He died the next year, aged 63.[8] Mordaunt, after the '59 rising joined the King and continued to cross and recross the Channel on royalist activities. He it was who took Monck's message secretly to Charles and brought back his reply. He was at Dover to welcome him and was created a Viscount for his tireless services.

The three brothers, Robert, Walter and Arthur Slingsby lived to see the Restoration. Robert, the oldest surviving sea-captain but unfit to serve abroad, received a baronetcy and was made Comptroller of the Navy, as his father had

169

been before him. Pepys talks of going to parties with him, bowling in his alley and playing the flageolet to him and Sir W. Penn one hot summer's evening in the garden, where they 'staid talking and singing and drinking great drafts of claret and eating botargo and bread and butter till 12 at night, it being moonshine; and so to bed, very near fuddled'.[9] The night he died, 26 October, 1664, Pepys could not sleep, 'he being a man that loved me, and had many qualitys that made me love him above all the other commissioners in the Navy' – one quality being his determination to check the wholesale corruption in the Navy Office.[10]

Walter became Deputy Governor of Carisbrooke Castle. Here he suspended the Postmaster of the Isle of Wight – 'a schismaticall knave put in by the Rump', guilty of intercepting his letters – and during the Dutch Wars sent Quaker conscientious objectors, who refused to pay their fines and were shut up in the Bridewell, the Koran to read 'for if it should turn them Turk it would be a great blow to the whole sect'.[11] He wrote accounts of some of the battles in the west for Clarendon to include in his History; and he told his cousin 'Samborne' that he had, for several years, been revising his brother, Guilford's, 'Narrative of Lord Strafford's arraignment and trial' and 'making such additions as are not only serving to illustrate the whole but to swell it up to a good folio', and that it was ready for the press. All he now needed was a licence to print, which he hoped 'Samborne' might be able to get for him.[12]

Arthur retired to his father's old house, Bifrons, near Canterbury, whence his wife, a Flemish lady, submitted a petition for a place as Lady of the Privy Chamber which had been promised her at Breda. She wrote that she 'had lost all her fortune in the King's service and left her country in confidence her husband's faithful service would give him employment'.[13] Arthur himself appealed for their son, the King's godson, to be a Page of Honour to the Queen at the next vacancy.[14] It was probably in an endeavour to relieve his want – a seemingly chronic state with most cavaliers – that he ran a lottery. Evelyn was one of the subscribers and went to watch the draw in the Banqueting House at Whitehall. 'I gained onely a trifle' he writes, 'as well as did the King, the Queen Consort and Queen Mother for neare 30 lotteries; which was thought to be contrived at very unhandsomely by the master of it, who was in truth a meer shark'. Pepys, characterisically enough, did not subscribe but was there, gazing on Lady Castlemaine and thinking it 'good sport to see how most that did give their two pounds did go away with a pair of gloves only for their lot'.[15] Arthur died at Bifrons in 1666 'of a sudden fit of vomiting'. He had been playing tennis at Whitehall only two days before.[16]

More popular with both Pepys and Evelyn was 'Samborne', Henry Slingsby, who became Master of the Mint in 1662 and one of the original members of the Royal Society. Evelyn talks of musical evenings at his house where his son and daughter, as well as 'the most renowned masters', performed;[17] and Pepys of dinners with him and discussion of coins and medals. He built a country house for himself in the peaceful village of Borough Green, near Newmarket, parts of which survive. But he was not able to enjoy it for long.[18] Official investigations revealed that he had not rendered accounts as Master of the Mint for the years 1662 – 1666, and 1670 – 1677, and in 1686 he had to surrender his patent. Four years later he died, still under a cloud, but it was a cloud of negligence, not dishonesty. Evelyn remained his loyal friend to the last and pleaded with 'the Lords of the Treasury to be favourable to him'.[19]

Lord Belasyse, who lived till 1689, was rewarded with the Lord Lieutenancy of the East Riding and the Governorship of Hull (where he was able to employ some of his Newark veterans). He also became Governor of the new colony of Tangier, where he spent a year. This put him in touch with Pepys whom he commended for his 'care and love to Tangier . . . and advice and constant correspondence which he valued'. Pepys took this to be 'a piece of courtship, yet it is a comfort to me that I am become so considerable as to have him need to say that to me.'[20] There is a monumental brass to Belasyse in St. Giles in the Fields where he is buried, but a more practical memorial is the 'hospital' he built at Worlaby for four poor widows as a thank offering for his safe return from the wars. These almshouses survive and give an idea of the architecture of Worlaby Hall which has long since disappeared.

Fauconberg, at the time of his uncle's execution, had just returned from France, whither he had borne letters from Cromwell to Louis XIV, and was having to entertain the French envoys in London as well as doing his utmost to save Slingsby and Hewitt. He and his wife left London as soon as they could after the execution and went up to Newburgh, the first time Mary had seen it. They were warmly and ceremoniously welcomed by all the neighbours and tenantry. Five years later they entertained the Duke of York and his Duchess (Clarendon's daughter) at Newburgh, to whose monastic peace Fauconberg had added his own love of books and gardens.[21] But the minds of those diners, in that particular house, may well have harboured disturbing thoughts. It were safer to forget the past. After Fauconberg's ambassadorship in Italy, trophies from which country adorn the house, he came to prefer his southern home, Sutton Court, Chiswick, and the music of his 'annual guests, the nightingales, to the noise of the jockeys at Newmarket'.[22] He died in 1697 and was buried in Coxwold church where his sumptuous monument occupies one wall of the chancel. Mary, whom Bishop Burnet called 'a wise and worthy woman, more likely to have maintained the post of Protector than either of her brothers', lived on till 1713 and was buried in Chiswick Church. She bore no children.

Sir Thomas Slingsby had married Dorothy Cradock two months after his father's execution – 'a very great wedding' wrote one guest; 'being one of the bride's kindred and friends, to avoid unkindness I went; since I kept no coach of my own six miles out of town going and coming was a great journey'.[23] We have seen the part he played in aiding the junction of Fairfax and Monck. As Lord Lieutenant of the West Riding, where a rising of the Fanatics was threatened in 1661, he took the precaution of securing York, for which his uncle, Lord Belasyse, Lord Lieutenant of the East Riding, commended him, suggesting that they kept in touch with each other by letter. In 1665 he too entertained the Duke and Duchess of York at Redhouse and, two years later, during the Dutch War was commissioned to raise a Troop of Horse. By 1670 he was Constable of Scarborough Castle and in '78 commanding a regiment in Flanders. Early the next year he was chosen M.P. for Knaresborough. His opponent, who had been 'drinking hard' against him, went on to drink harder for York. He died in 1688, leaving three sons and two daughters.[24] It seems he was never as close to his father as Henry had been, and it is perhaps significant that it was not he, but his son, Thomas, who 35 years after the execution had the black marble stone inscribed and placed over Sir Harry's grave. As heir to the estates he had possibly been critical of his father's 'pertinacity' which all but broke them up.

Henry became a Gentleman of the Privy Chamber and one of the first members of the council of the Royal Society. He served in the Royal Regiment of Horse and became its Colonel in 1688.[25] He was also a Gentleman of the Bedchamber to James II and Governor of, and M.P. for, Portsmouth. Barbara, his sister, had in 1660 married Sir John Talbot of Lacock Abbey where their portraits, and that of her father, still hang. Talbot had been too young to fight in the war, but became the Worcestershire leader of the plots in the south-west to restore Charles, for which he was imprisoned. There is a tradition that he rushed to Dover in May 1660 and was the first to hand the King ashore. He was knighted in June and in the ensuing years Barbara bore him two sons (both of whom died young) and three daughters. In the Dutch War of 1667 his regiment of foot was ordered to Chatham in readiness for another attempt by the Dutch, at the next spring tides, to sail up the Medway.[26] In 1671 he was M.P. for Chippenham.

Slingsby, who had charged his sons to be 'diligent in the vocation or imployment you are called unto, and be ever doing some good work, that the devil may never find you unimployed', could rest content.

The last of the Slingsbys was Sir Charles who was drowned in the hunting accident already mentioned. On his death Redhouse passed to his sister and from her, since she had no heir, to the Reverend Charles Atkinson, who assumed the name of Slingsby. He broke his neck in 1912 in the hunting field near Thickpenny Farm, half a mile from Redhouse, and the school groom who, out riding with a boy that day, had holloaed the fox away from Redhouse Wood, never forgave himself. This 'man of the field and a faithful priest' as the Archbishop of York described him, was buried at Moor Monkton. The sensational Slingsby Baby Case followed soon after his death, the baby being the son and heir of Lt.-Cdr. Charles Slingsby and his American wife, then living in Vancouver, B.C. The Commander's brothers and sister always believed that this child, born in San Francisco, was a changeling and proceeded to challenge its legitimacy. After intensive investigation of all the circumstances surrounding the alleged birth of the baby the case was heard in the Probate and Divorce Court and the family's suspicions seemed fully justified. Mrs Slingsby was said, by the nurse living with her at the time, to have had a miscarriage and to have adopted the baby son of a Hawaiian schoolgirl. This was denied by Mrs Slingsby who further denied, on oath, that she had ever advertised in a local paper for a baby to adopt. On being confronted with the advertisement in her own handwriting, she admitted that she had done this because she had been afraid of another miscarriage, having had several in the past. Even the birth certificate had been wrong in three particulars — the place of birth, the mother's age and the father's name. But the case ended, early in 1915, in favour of the chubby curly-haired three-year-old who appeared in court, chiefly on the strength of resemblances noticed by Sir George Frampton (the eminent R.A., sculptor of Peter Pan) between the boy's and the father's peculiarly shaped jaw, and the boy's and his mother's peculiarly shaped left ear. Pictures of father, mother and son, full-face to display the jaw, side-face to display the ear, appeared in 'The Tatler' as winners of the case. One daily paper showed pictures of Scriven and Redhouse, the future residences of the Slingsbys.

The rest of the family were not going to take this lying down and in 1916 brought an appeal, which they won. At the end of the year the Commander appealed against this judgment but, in view of the shadiness of most of the witnesses and their contradictory evidence, especially that of the principal and perjured, witness, Mrs Slingsby herself, lost his appeal and was saddled with costs. The pictures that had appeared in 'The Tatler' now reappeared in 'The Sphere', but in the role of 'losers of the Slingsby Drama'. So the estates, saved from confiscation 300 years before by the financial efforts of relatives, were now swallowed up by the law, and Redhouse, which the headmaster had at one time been warned he would have to vacate to provide a summer residence for the Commander and his family, was put up for sale and became his property.

1   Pepys, 23 April 1661.
2   Cobbett, State Trials, V, 1265.
3   Ludlow, Memoirs, 369–70.
4   HMC V Report App. 208.
5   CSPD 1661–2, 232.
6   HMC Buccleuch II. 49
7   HMC Ormonde, New Series VII, 410.
8   F. H. Sunderland, 230.
9   Pepys, 5 June 1661.
10 Pepys, 26 October 1661.
11 CSPD 1664–6, 108–9.
12 HMC VI Report, 340.
13 CSPD 1661–2, 29.
14 CSPD 1663–4, 34.
15 Pepys 20 July 1664.
16 HMC VI Report 337b.
17 Evelyn IV.
18 Cambridge Antiquarian Society Proceedings 1939, W. M. Palmer, 26–33.
19 Evelyn IV. 567.
20 Pepys, 13th January 1665.
21 HMC Mrs Frankland-Russell-Astley, 47. Writing to his brother-in-law, Sir William Frankland, Fauconberg says, 'If the pears I sent you come just ripe there is no such fruit in the world. To eat for 3 months together a fruit more delicate than the best peach or fig at midsummer commends a garden and makes me resolve to plant nothing but pears henceforth . . . This pain I take only to make you as good a gardener as myself'. 10 Nov 1681.

22 HMC Mrs Frankland-Russell-Astley. But he still went to Newmarket for on 6 April 1682 he wrote 'I could not return by Cambridge, being certainly informed that the Master and Fellows of Trinity College were prepared to attack me with a speech for a subscription to their new Library and building, which I could not have honourably avoided'.

23 HMC V Report, 146.

24 HMC Mrs Frankland-Russell-Astley, 41.

25 Dalton, 'English Army List', 5. 178.

26 Diary, 373.

Appendix I

Sir Henry Slingsby's Will, made in the Tower June 4th
1658

My will and desire is that my daughter Barbary Slingesby
have for her portion all that money in Sir John Fenwick's
hands according to a deal made her thereof, and all that
money Brian Stapylton of Myton Esquire had or has of
mine and also desire my son Thomas Slingsby Esquire may
have the lands about Knaresborough which I surrendered
to the use of my daughter Barbary Slingesby surrendered to
him again and that the lease made to my said daughter for
life of a certain close above Knaresborough shall be void if
my said son Thomas Slingesby shall pay unto my said
daughter Barbary the sum of £1500 any tyme within a
twelve month otherwise the above said surrender and leave
made to my said daughter Barbary are hereby by me
intended to be conferred to her.

I also desire my son Thomas Slingesby will give to my son
Henry Slingesby the somme of £2500 pounds within a
year after the date here if my said son Thomas shall not
marry within a year of the date hereof I desire he will pay
my son Henry the yearly rent of £100 till he my said son
Thomas shall marry the first payment thereof to be paid to
my said son Henry at Michelmas which shall be in the
year '58.

I also desire my said son Thomas Slingesby to paye my
said son Henry Slingesby £2500 within 6 months after my
said son Thomas Slingesby's marriage whenever it shall
happen to bee and that upon payment of the said £2500 to
my son Henry as above said all deeds and writings whatsoever made for his my said son Henry's provision may be

cancelled delivered up to my said son Thomas.

I desire my said son Thomas may have the 100 pounds for which he has Mr John . . . and others bounde for my funeral expenses and that my body may be carried to Knaresborough church and there buried in the grave already prepared.

I desire that my said son Thomas do give my servants Will Smith 10 pounds and Thomas Adamson 40s. and to consider them as faithful old servants to me.

I desire and charge my son Thomas Slingesby to do and performe all things above said and do hereby give unto him my son Thomas all my personal estate whatsoever excepting that above given and do hereby revoke and declare null all other wills whatever in witness whereof I have hereunto putte my hande this 4th day of June 1658.

Henry Slingesby.

Copy of Major-General Sir James Lumsden's letter
to Lord Loudon.

These are to give your Lordship accompt of the victorie it hath pleased God to bestow on us far above our deserts, and the way was thus. Prince Rupert advancing for York we brak up our beleaguring to meet him, he haiffing ane order which was intercepted from the King, that nothing but Impossibilities should stay him from beating the Scots. As we were marching he put the river Ewes betwixt us so that he came to York without any stope, so that we lay four myles therefrom, and on the morrow we brak up to march to Tadcaster to attend his retreat. Our foot haiffing the vanne we were not 1 myle from it; the alarme was sent us by our horss that Prince Rupert was with his wholl armie advancing which mad us presently march bak to the bounds we had left, where we found him drawing up in ane plain feild 3 myles in length and in breidth, the fairest ground for such use that I had seen in England. We finding him so neir and no possibilitie to have up our foot in two hours, keepedt the advantage of ane sleeke and the hills with our horss till the foot as they came up were put in order. In the meantyme we advanced our canon and entred to play on them on the left wing, which maid them a littell to move; which they persaving brocht up thairs and gave us the lyk. This continued not long when it was resolved we should advance down the hill throch ane great feild of corne to ane ditch which they had in possession, which it pleased God so to prosper that they wer put from it, so that the service went on verie hot on all sydes, we lossing on the right wing and gaining on the left. They that faucht stood extraordinarie weill to it; whereof my Lord Lyndsay, his brigad commandit by himself, was one. These brigads that failyied on the vanne wer presently supplied by Cassilis, Kilheid, Cowper, Dumfermling and some of Cliddisdaills regiment who wer on the battel, and gained what they had lost, and maid themselffs masters of the cannon was nixt to them, and tooke Sir Charles Lucas, Leivetenant Generall of their horss, prisoner. These that ran away shew themselffs most baselie. I commanding the battel was on the heid of your Lordship's regiment and Buccleuches but they carryed not themselffs as I would have wissed, nather could I prevaill with them. For these that fled never came to chairge with the enemies, but wer so possessed with ane pannik fear that they ran for example to others and no enemie following, which gave the enemie occasioun to chairge them, they intendit not, and they had only the loss. We have only Lord Dudope prisoner, and Livetennant Collonel Bryson is killed, 2 capitans and some souldiers. We have Sir Charles Lucas, General major Porter, some collonels and other officers, with sundrie of their cheiff officers killed. The number killed to the enemie as is esteimed is 2000 and above, with 1500 prisoers, 20 peice of canon which wer all they had, all ther ammunition, all ther baggage, 10,000 armes, all ther foot colours, many cornets. The horss on our right wing wer beat, my Lord Eglintoun not being well seconded. Sir Thomas Fairfax commandit thair in cheiff, ane brave commander, but his horss answered not our expectatioun, nor his worth; they gave some blame to the commandit musqueteris wer with them My Lord Eglintoun commandit our horss there who shew himself weill, his son releiving his father who was far engagded is evill wounded. Our left wing of horss which was commandit by Livetennant Generall Cromwell and Generall major David Leslie carryed themselffs bravelie, and under God was ane main occasioun for our victorie. I must not overpass Manchester's foot, who did good service under the command of Generall major Crawford, our Generall being cheiff commander himself, Livetennant Generall Baillie commandit the vanne of ours under him and Fairfax and Manchesters of their own. So your Lordship . . . the brigads drawn up heir . . . not so formall as it ought to be . . . Your Lordship's most humble servant J. Lumsden in our leaguer at York the 5 of July 1644. This letter is directed to my . . . by Sir James Lumsden . . . is a just copie'.

Uponn the left their was 3000 horss of the erle of Manchesters commandit by his Livetennant generall Cromwell and we had 1000 horss commandit by generall major Leslie with the intervall of musqueteirs.
The enemies strength as their awin Livetennant generall affirms was 7000 Horss and 1200 foot.

(a.a.) . . . . . Maitland their reg(iment)
b.(b.) . . . . . artilearie and . . . .
c.(c.) . . . . . (Fai)rfax
dd.ee. Belonging to M(anchester)
f.f. To Lord Chancellor & Bu(ccleugh)
g.g. . . . . . (Ca)ssillis and Ke(lheid)
h.(h.) . . . . (Du)mfermling and Co(wper)
j.j. . . . . Levingstoun and Y(e)ster
k.k. Lord M(anchester)
l.l. Lord Dudope and . . . . (E)rskyne
m.m.n.n. Lord (Fairfa)x both . . . . .
o.o. . . . . anchtoun . . . . .

Upon the richt of horss 500 draguners, betwixt everie squadron of horss 50 musqueteirs marked with the letter P. The Lord Fairfax had on his wing 3000 horss under the command of his sone Sir Thomas generall major and with them on the same hand we had 1000 horss commandit by the Lord Eglintoun.

The reproduction of this letter is by kind permission of Mr H. L. Verry, C.B.E., who discovered it in a London antiquarian bookshop; and to Brigadier Peter Young, who purchased it from him.

Appendix II

(see caption on frontispiece)

The inscription, written under a red seal on what looks like a scroll, reads :

> An unhappie President
> In armis Jura dicere
> Et omnia Fortium
> virorum esse
> ∴ Aetat 53 1655 ∴

This may be translated thus : "An unhappy precedent to pronounce judgment in arms, and for all things to belong to the strong". This must be another of Slingsby's Latin aphorisms, directed this time against the rule of Cromwell and the army into whose hands he either had already fallen, or was soon to fall. For in March 1655, the year the picture was presumably painted, he took part in that ill-fated rising for which he was arrested and subsequently tried in York Castle. The barred window, immediately above the inscription, adds poignancy to the inscription.

Bibliography

ORIGINAL SOURCES

ABBOT, W. C. – *The Writings and Speeches of Oliver Cromwell*
ASSHETON, NICHOLAS – *Journal of,* (Chetham Society)
BURTON, THOMAS – *Diary of*
ADDITIONAL MANUSCRIPTS – British Museum
BARWICK, DR. JOHN – *Life of*
CALENDAR OF CLOSE ROLLS
CALENDAR OF PATENT ROLLS
CARTE, T. – *A Collection of Original Letters, etc.,* 1641-1660
CLARKE PAPERS – *ed. C. H. Firth,* Camden Society
CLARENDON – *Calendar of State Papers*
CLARENDON – *MSS*
CLARENDON – *History of the Rebellion & Civil Wars in England*
CLARENDON, EDWARD, EARL OF – *The Life of & Continuation of his History*
CLARENDON, EDWARD, EARL OF – *State Papers collected by*
CALENDAR OF THE PROCEEDINGS OF THE COMMITTEE FOR COMPOUNDING
CALENDAR OF STATE PAPERS, DOMESTIC SERIES 1649-1660
COATE, M. – *The Letter-Book of John, Viscount Mordaunt* 1658-1660
EVELYN'S DIARY
FAIRFAX CORRESPONDENCE
FOLGER MS xd 428 – Folger Shakespeare Library, Washington D.C.
HISTORICAL MANUSCRIPTS COMMISSION
HOWELL, T. B. & T. J. – *A Complete Collection of State Trials,* vol 5
LUDLOW'S MEMOIRS
MERCURIUS AULICUS
MERCURIUS POLITICUS
MONCKTON PAPERS
NICHOLAS, SIR EDWARD – Secretary of State, Correspondence of: *The Nicholas Papers*
PEPYS'S DIARY
PERFECT DIURNALL
PERFECT PROCEEDINGS
LIFE OF THE RENOWNED DR. PRESTON – *writ by his pupil Thomas Ball, D.D. minister of Northampton in* 1628
RAWLINSON MS – (Bodleian)
ROYALIST COMPOSITION PAPERS

SLINGSBY, SIR HENRY – *Diary of*
SURTEES SOCIETY – *Yorkshire Diaries*
TRIAL OF MR MORDAUNT – *or the Pretended High Court of Justice in West-minster Hall,* 1 and 2 *June* 1658 by T. W.
THURLOE'S STATE PAPERS
TWYSDEN, SIR ROGER – *Journal: Archaeologia Cantiana, vol. IX*
WARWICK, SIR PHILIP – *Memoirs of*
WHITELOCKE – *Memorials*
WHITAKER, DR. – *History of Whalley* (Chetham Society)

SECONDARY SOURCES

BATESON – *History of Northumberland*
BIRKENHEAD – *Strafford*
CAMBRIDGE ANTIQUARIAN SOCIETY – *Proceedings* (1939)
CARTWRIGHT, J. J. – *Chapters on the History of Yorkshire*
COLLINS PEERAGE – *ed.* Sir Egerton Brydges
COOK, SIR THEODORE – *History of the English Turf*
DRAKE – *Eboracum*
ENGLISH HISTORICAL REVIEW
ESDAILE – *English Church Monuments*
FIRTH, C. H. – *The Royalists under the Protectorate*
FULLER – *The History of the Worthies of England*
GARDINER, S. R. – *History of the Commonwealth & the Protectorate*
GENT – *History of Hull*
GIBB, M. A. – *The Lord General*
GRANGER – *Biographies*
GRAY, J. H. – *History of the Queen's College*
HARGROVE, E. – *History of Knaresborough*
HARTE – *Life of Gustavus Adolphus*
HARLEIAN SOCIETY – *Yorkshire Pedigrees*
HEATH, CHARLES – *History & Descriptive Account of Raglan Castle*
HOBMAN – *Cromwell's Master Spy*
HOLLOND – *Discourses of the Navy*
JOSEPH – *Yorkshire Pedigrees*
KEELER, M. – *Long Parliament*
LLOYD, D. – *Memoirs of the Lives of the Noble Persons etc.*
MARKHAM – *A Life of the Great Lord Fairfax*
MCMASTER, J. – *A Short History of St. Martins-in-the-Fields*
MORGAN, I. – *Prince Charles' Puritan Chaplains*
NOBLE – *Lives of the Regicides*
PEARSON, HESKETH – *The Smith of Smiths*
PENNANT – *Tours to and from Alston Moor*
PEVSNER – *Yorkshire, West Riding; Lincolnshire*
POULSON – *History of the Antiquities of Holderness*
PRIOR, C. M – *The Royal Studs in the 16th and 17th Centuries*

RAMSEY, R. W. – *Studies in Oliver Cromwell's Family Circle*
RANNIE, D. W. – *Cromwell's Major-Generals*
RECKITT, B. N. – *Charles I & Hull*
SCOTT, EVA – *The Travels of the King*
SHEAHAN – *History of Hull*
SUNDERLAND, F. H. – *Marmaduke, Lord Langdale*
TICKELL – *History of Hull*
UNDERDOWN, D. – *Royalist Conspiracy in England*
UPTON, A. – *Sir Arthur Ingram*
VARLEY, F. J. – *Oxford in the Civil War*
WEDGWOOD, C. V. – *The King's War, The Trial of Charles I*
WHEATER – *Some Historic Mansions of Yorkshire*
YORKSHIRE ARCHAEOLOGICAL JOURNAL

Index

191